Adrift
in the Digital Age

A Brief Look at Parenting in the New Millennium

Adrift
in the Digital Age

A Brief Look at Parenting
in the New Millennium

James Mehegan, Ph.D.

STANDISH ROAD BOOKS

Editor – Nancy Benjamin
Design and Production – Janis Owens, janisowensdesign.com

ISBN: 9781733885607

Library of Congress Control Number: 2019903607

PRINTED IN THE UNITED STATE OF AMERICA

To the hundreds of dedicated parents who formulated plans,
tried them, revised them, and tried again.

To the hundreds of young people who told me when we got
it right, and told me when we got it wrong, and told me why.

To Christopher, Tyler, and Kelsey,
always just a keystroke away.

And most of all, to Diane, who encouraged and supported
and finally talked me into writing it all down.

Contents

Introduction
Adrift in the Digital Age

In most ways, the task of parenting in the digital age is the same as it always has been: giving to our children the gift of roots when they are young, and the gift of wings when they are older. The basic concept is not particularly complicated. In the early years, we provide a foundation by keeping our children safe, and providing them with a stable home and a clear road map to distinguish right from wrong. In later years, we encourage these same children to take that foundation out into the world, and use it to guide their behavior. The relative emphasis on one of these goals versus the other evolves over the years, and this evolution leads to some extraordinarily difficult decisions. Is it, for example, our primary goal to keep a sixteen-year-old safe (at the expense of developing the ability to make autonomous decisions in difficult situations), or to allow more independence and more opportunity to learn from mistakes (at the risk of dangerous behavior)? It's one thing to have this dilemma with a young child learning to ride a bike, when the downside risk is scraping a knee. It's another entirely when the downside risk is pregnancy, drug addiction, or death. It's no wonder that most conscientious parents are a lot better at roots than at wings. This has always been true, and will never change.

The digital age does, however, provide a variety of entirely novel challenges. Take, for example, the simple matter of finding out what's going on in the world. Not that long ago, this wasn't a big deal. Network news was on the TV at 6 p.m., and you tuned in from time to time. If you read a newspaper, you knew that the front page was news, and the editorial page was opinion — or at least you knew that it was the responsibility of the editors to make that distinction. And that was pretty much it. Now, the world of news assaults you twenty-four hours a day and has become as polarized as the world of politics. Everyone has an agenda. Information is shaped, spun, monetized, and weaponized, and there is nowhere to turn to simply find out what's going on. We'll return to this topic later, but for now just consider the fact that a substantial percentage of people get all their news from social media, which makes no attempt whatsoever to figure out what's real. This is the world in which we are raising our children, and our survival as a representative democracy depends on these children being able to intelligently discriminate truth from lies, and opinion from news. And since no one else is going to do something about this, it falls to us.

And this just scratches the surface of the impact of the internet on parenting. Who tells you how much video gaming is too much? Or at what age to give your child a cell phone?

Or what access to allow to social media? Or whether to put controls on your router? Or how to make and enforce sensible rules around any of these topics?

Whether or not the internet is involved, there can be no simple guide to the countless decisions we make through the course of the parenting journey, because the "correct" answer for your child can vary by age, maturity, family dynamics, and a host of other variables. In addition, the pace of technological change guarantees that there is no way to know how these decisions will show up next week, let alone a decade from now. I can promise you this: your children will find ways to confront you with decisions for which you will not be prepared. The truth is that hardly a week goes by in my practice that I'm not presented with something I've never heard before. No resource could possibly prepare you for every situation you will face.

However, all is most assuredly not lost. On the contrary, the core techniques of parenting, like its core philosophy, remain the same: loving, and limit setting. That's it. Limit setting in the context of love is how you move from roots to wings. Love your children, no matter how difficult that may be at times. And learn basic behavioral technology, so that you can effectively and consistently set limits based on your value system. The principle is easy. The execution of the principle is, I will grant you, a challenge.

"Basic behavioral technology," for example, is not a lot of fun to learn, and you'll be tempted to just skip ahead to a particular issue you're having in your family. I don't blame you. But stick with me through Chapter One, if you can, because you'll find that the concepts reappear over and over in different forms through all the stages we'll be discussing, and I promise you they're worth learning. For one thing, the behavioral approach works. That's a good thing. For another, it keeps the focus on the here and now. To be a good behavior manager, you don't need to understand every nuance of developmental theory, and you don't need to beat yourself up about your historical role in your child's current problems. You just need to figure out what to do next. An overall sense of what our main goals are, and an idea of how to structure a behavioral plan, should get us through most of the interesting events. The plan is to get the techniques straight long before the digital stuff is an issue. Which makes sense, because not that many infants have tablets or smart phones. Yet.

I will also do my best to steer clear of political and sociological controversies, if that is possible in today's world. It's not my business to tell you what your values should be, but rather to help you craft a family system that supports your beliefs, whatever they may be. Of course I have opinions, and they'll probably leak through, but I'm not going to parse every word here in an attempt to be politically correct. Stylistically, for example, I will not be consistent in my use of pronouns: sometimes I'll use "he" and sometimes "she." Don't worry about it. Most of what we talk about applies to everyone, regardless of gender or, indeed, gender identity. If I generalize without always noting the exceptions, it's not because I don't know that they exist. The goal here is to be useful to parents, not to get caught up in political, philosophical, or semantic arguments. If we raise confident, grounded kids, they can figure out their own politics when they get older.

The simple fact is that most of us get at best a couple of chances to try out this parenting thing. By the time we have some idea of what we're doing, our kids move on, and the next generation of parents is required to reinvent the wheel. Or else we figure out how to handle a boy, and then we get a girl. Or else we figure out how to handle a young girl, and then she becomes a teenager. It's hard to step back from the flow of family life and make sense of it all, because it seems to go by so quickly. So, as I noted above, I've tried in these pages to condense what I think I've learned over the years about what works and what doesn't, what's important and what isn't, and why it all matters. My hope is that it will help you to understand what is happening in your own family, and to alter it, if you decide it's necessary.

Before getting started, though, let's talk about the most useful attitude and approach to bring to the task of parenting. It is certainly true that each phase of child rearing can be difficult in its own way. However, each one can be rewarding in its own way as well. If you enter the process with the preconception that the twos will be terrible, or that all teenagers are a horror show, or any of the various other dire assumptions that pass for wisdom and experience in our society, then you'll increase your chances of finding what you expect. It is certainly true that raising children is one of the most difficult things we do. However, it is also, for most of us, our signature task in life, and the one most telling about our character. It is time-consuming, exhausting, mostly thankless, entirely unpaid — and totally worth the effort. The job we do has the unique capacity to echo down the corridors of time, as our children treat others in accordance with the template we have provided. In short, doing the absolute best we can at parenting is almost as much a calling as it is a job. In a society that seems to value material wealth above all else, it is well to remember this. If you go into it planning to give, and expecting nothing in return (as good a working definition of love as I've ever heard), you'll be fine.

A final note about attitude, with specific reference to behavior management. You may recall having had a substitute teacher when you were in grade school. Question: how long did it take you and your classmates to figure out whether this was one of those adults who was going to be in control of your class, or whether this was one of those you were going to dominate? When I ask this question, most people respond that it took a matter of seconds — if that long. When an adult is in control, a child knows it. When an adult is lost, a child knows that, too. All the behavioral technology in the world won't help you if you haven't thought through what your fundamental goals and values are, if you are not confident in your long-term plan, and if you don't know what the rules are in your own home. You don't need to get every single interaction right. Which is a good thing, because no one does. But you do need to develop and broadcast the confidence that you know what your family stands for, and that you will be calm and firm and relentless in pursuit of family interactions that reflect those beliefs. There's nothing magical about this. If you face your children with the calm certainty that you are in control, then you probably will be. If you fear that they will disobey and that you won't be in control, then you probably won't be. Assume that from time to time you'll make plans that won't work. No big deal. Think it through, and make a new plan for tomorrow.

It may also be useful to comment briefly on where the role of parent fits into a functioning marriage — although certainly an entire book could be devoted to the topic. All successful marriages have as an essential element the fundamental assumption that the role of each spouse is equally important and equally valued. If there is an unspoken calculus going on behind the scenes regarding which spouse is doing more, the marriage is in trouble. The two of you will end up competing for who's the most miserable. Which is stupid. Having a job and earning money is hard and often stressful. Likewise, raising children is hard and often stressful. From the former, you usually get evenings and weekends and vacations when there's a break from work. From the latter, you get none of these. From the former, you get pay and perhaps recognition, but at least opportunities to interact with adults. From the latter, you get none of these. Both tasks are essential, and both must be done. I am taking no position here on the question of men versus women in the role of caregiver, nor am I commenting on the case of both parents working. I am simply suggesting that in many marriages, both parents feel overworked, and have the uncomfortable and corrosive sense that perhaps they are working harder than their spouse. This invariably results in anger, misunderstandings, and resentment, and needs to be talked through. Traditionally, the job of parent (and house-keeper) has been spectacularly undervalued, usually by men (but sometimes by women as well, especially in recent years). Anger and resent in a marriage steals energy from the tasks at hand. The best bet is for *both* spouses to assume that the *other* is working harder and to act accordingly. Then you'll take care of each other. Then it will work.

In addition, I cannot state strongly enough that reasonable amounts of time must be set aside for self-care and for care of the marital relationship. And both must be planned and scheduled, or else they will not happen; the spontaneity you depended on before you had children is a thing of the past. I can't tell you how often I speak with couples who no longer do anything with each other for fun, and who then wonder why they seem to have a joyless marriage. If you always "put the children first" at the expense of self-care and care of the marriage, you won't have the energy to do a good job, and the marriage will wither. Which is bad for the children. If you are depressed and you don't seek out help (or even fun) for your-self, you won't have the energy to do a good job, and *you* will wither. Which is bad for the children. Admittedly, in the years of child rearing, there won't be as much time either for your-self or for your marital relationship as you would wish. But it doesn't have to be zero. What you signed up for when you had children is to use your time more efficiently and to no longer depend on spontaneity to meet your needs and those of your marriage. If, for some unfathomable reason, you are reading this before you have children, these would be good things to think about before you do. Sometimes, when I'm doing

marital therapy, I think to myself that even if I'm totally useless as a therapist, at least the couple I'm seeing has to make
a date to be together at the same time, not doing chores, and
without the children.

As a culture, I think we've gotten out of balance. You don't
need to start planning your child's college resume when
he's in the womb. He's probably not going to be the second
coming of Mozart or Babe Ruth, and starting him with music
lessons or private coaching at the age of four isn't going to
alter that fact. Kids and their caretakers are so overbooked,
overplanned, and overcommitted that no one is having any
fun. But since everyone else is doing it, you feel like you're
putting your kid at a disadvantage if you don't. Relax already.
There's no real evidence that all this intensity makes that
much difference in the long run. Sports and music and art
and dance and all the rest are supposed to be for enjoyment.
Get too intense and they're not enjoyable anymore. Mix some
of them in, sure. (As we'll mention later, some of these arenas
will provide good forums for success, and therefore are useful
for building self-esteem.) But not multiple sports and multiple instruments and multiple leagues all at the same time.
Read to your child, sure. For the fun of it. Not to drill her
on spelling and phonics. And you don't need to go to every
game, every practice, every event. You don't need to entertain
her every moment, and you don't need to spend a zillion dollars on programs and tutors and, God help us, toddler music
classes. Parenting like this is a drag. And, if you want to know
the truth, so is childing. (I doubt that's a word, but you know
what I mean.) In fact, if you aren't careful, you'll end up with

an anxious child who worries that she doesn't measure up to expectations, won't get into the "right" college, and will never succeed at life. And then you'll have to call a child psychologist. Who will hopefully remind you that happiness in life has much more to do with the quality of relationships you have than the college you went to, your salary, or your social class. And who will also hopefully remind you that the best way to engender those relationships is through the gentle and consistent expression of love and setting of limits in the home.

There's my soapbox on that topic. It's just my opinion. Lots of people disagree with me. You can think it through and figure out what to do in your family.

A final technical note: I had the choice when I was writing this to either follow the topic at hand as it emerged through the years, or follow the chronological age of the children and come back to topics as they came up over time. I chose the latter, but the result is that you'll find I'm constantly saying "we'll come back to this later" in these pages. Which might drive you a bit nuts. But it's a better choice than the "age jumping" that the other approach would have required. I think, in most cases, I actually *do* return to the topic. You can be the judge of that.

Behavioral Principles
The Basics

Let's set all the digital stuff aside for a bit to have a look at some central behavioral principles, and see how they can be used to achieve our goals in both the short and long terms. Then we'll follow the application of these ideas in (more or less) chronological order through the child-rearing years. I should start by saying that I've spoken with many parents who have said to me, in one form or another, "I've tried that behavioral stuff, and it doesn't work." I always wonder what they imagine there might be *other* than behavioral stuff, because the fact is that we are using behavioral techniques all the time, whether or not we call them by that name. Spanking is a behavioral technique. So are guilt tripping, ignoring, lecturing, encouraging, and everything else in the parenting arsenal. All families have a curriculum, and all families are always teaching something. It's just that most parents don't know how to take apart what they are teaching; they are disorganized and inconsistent, and end up teaching things they never intended to convey. A familiarity with behavioral principles allows you to sort out what exactly the curriculum is in your family and to ensure that it's the one that you intended.

In addition, a behavioral perspective is nonjudgmental. It doesn't seek to blame current problems on anyone or anything from the past. That is not to say that the "whys" of behavior aren't interesting and sometimes worth exploring. But it's not always necessary to know why a child is doing something to figure out what to do about it. Usually, by the way, the underlying reason is a lot simpler than a deeply buried trauma emerging symbolically as dysfunctional behavior that can only be unraveled by a skilled psychotherapist in long-term therapy (although that makes a good movie plot). In the long run, it's not very useful to blame either yourself or your child for whatever problems you may be having. Most parents do their best. Most children want to be successful and loved. You just need to figure out what to do today, not where it all came from, or where it may be headed. In fact, worrying about those things will make it harder for you to keep your emotions out of the behavior management process — a task, as we will discuss in detail, that is critical. For now, however, let's turn to some specific and frequently misunderstood behavioral language.

Start with the words "punishment" and "reinforcement." In behavioral psychology, these words have very specific meanings. A punisher decreases the frequency of a target behavior in a particular set of circumstances. A reinforcer, in contrast, increases the likelihood of the target behavior. Like many behavioral concepts, these are simple, but their implications are complex. Here, for example, is a conversation I've had dozens of times:

> **Parent:** He's constantly breaking the rule.
> **Me:** Do you punish him?
> **Parent:** Yes, but it doesn't change anything. He still breaks the rule.
> **Me:** Then what you used wasn't a punisher. You didn't punish him.

On the face of it, this seems like such a simple observation. But in practice it's not always obvious. We have in our minds what we think is punishment, so we apply it after misbehavior. We give our children, for example, a stern "talking to," and nothing changes. Why not? It may be that some children like the attention. It may be that some just tune us out. In any case (and note that you don't need to figure out the underlying dynamic), if you applied what you thought was a punisher after a behavior and it didn't decrease the frequency of the target behavior, then, by definition, it wasn't a punisher. Simple as that. If you are thinking like a behaviorist, you cannot possibly say, "I punished him, but he's still doing it just as often." Instead, you might say, "I thought I was punishing him. Turns out I was wrong." And if you "punish" a child and the behavior doesn't decrease, that's not the fault of the child. It just means that you didn't understand what, in his world, is a punisher. No need to be angry about this; just step back and rethink it. After all, the goal of behavioral intervention is behavior change, not revenge.

The classic example of this principle takes place in the classroom, where a teacher may focus the most attention on the worst-behaved children, with the assumption that angry attention is a punisher. For some children, of course, this may be true, and the target behavior may decrease. But if, for whatever reason, attention itself is a powerful enough reinforcer to overcome the potency of anger as a punisher, then the target behavior may increase, not decrease. But this scenario is a step more complex than that, because the well-behaved children get ignored while the poorly behaved children are getting disciplined. Let's assume that attention from the teacher is a powerful reinforcer for some of the well-behaved children as well. In that case, what you are also teaching is that to get attention, you need to misbehave. This is, of course, the exact opposite of what the teacher intends the classroom curriculum to be. But this curriculum is not obvious unless you learn to step back, think through the reinforcers and punishers, and figure out what is really being taught. As we will see, this is exactly the skill you need to develop as a parent.

I'm going to take a relatively extensive philosophical detour here, to emphasize what may be the most important point I make in this entire book. You will hear it explicitly in some contexts, and it lies implicitly behind yet others. It is this: any time you get angry in the process of behavior management, you have failed as a behavior manager. This is because if you become angry, then whatever is going on is no longer about the target behavior. It's about love or hate or your relationship with your child or guilt or any of a host of other unpredictable psychological variables. Managing behavior calmly and dispassionately, especially in the face of some of the creatively defiant and annoying behaviors in our children's behavioral repetoires, is a huge challenge. But that's how you keep the focus on the behavior. Your child is not being punished because you are angry. He is being punished because he broke a rule. He is not being punished because you are tired or are having a bad day or are mad at your spouse (all of which may be true as well, of course), but because he broke a rule. You are saying this: "If you don't like the punishment, don't break the rule." Simple. Of course, your child will try to drag emotion into the issue. He will say "I hate you" or "you never punish my brother," or "no other parent in the known universe is as strict as you," or today's wildly infuriating and utterly scornful "whatever." This is perfectly natural, because the more your child can drag you into the swamp of emotionality, the more power he has in the situation — and children seek power within the family structure as naturally as they breathe. But if you keep your cool, deflect all the drama, and stay focused on the problematic behavior, you will be teaching what you intend to teach: "Break this rule, and you will get this result." Or, to phrase it more generally: "Actions have consequences. If you don't want the consequences, don't perform the action." (We'll come back to this in a moment.) Clearly, this is one of the most important lessons we impart through the years, and we get plenty of opportunities to do it. Equally clearly, no parent gets this right every time. You'll get angry. You'll get dragged in. You'll say the stupid stuff you promised you'd never say, back when your parents said it to you, like "because I said so." You'll blow it sometimes. We all do. You can get better.

But there is a second equally important issue at hand. Remember that even though we, in the moment, are managing a specific problem, ultimately, we are teaching *self*-control. We are teaching that, not just at home but in the wider world, actions have consequences. If you punish because you are angry, then the event is at least in part about your anger, and the lesson you end up teaching is to not get caught — to misbehave more cleverly. But if your business as a parent is to impart values, the whole idea is that you are teaching your children to adhere to those values *whether or not* anyone is looking over their shoulder. You are saying that there are right and wrong ways to behave that transcend whatever specific behavior may be the issue at that moment. You are saying that this is how good people behave. Lessons such as these are not learned in the context of anger.

Now it is true that if we are going to teach our children values through the medium of rules, they will, from time to time, be angry at us. Many times, actually. But it is not our job, as parents, to avoid their anger. On the contrary, we should assume that some degree of conflict is both necessary and productive. Limits in the context of love is how values are learned. Here is the message in its simplest form:

> Yes, I love you.
> No, you can't do that.

Here's another way to look at it: it is not our job to have our teenagers think we're the coolest parents on the block. It is our job to be able to look them in the eye when they are twenty-five and say, "I always made the best parenting decisions I was able to make, even when you said you hated me."

In summary, keep in mind that we are up to two things here. On the one hand, we are establishing and enforcing rules that make our homes function more smoothly. And at a higher level, we are providing an externally imposed set of limits in keeping with our own value systems, which we hope our children will eventually internalize, turn into their own values, and use to guide their future behavior. Ultimately, of course, it is this second part that is more important, because they'll spend many more years without us than they will with us. So how do we maximize the chance that this will happen?

This question brings us back to the issue of the nature of the relationship we have with our children. As we have noted, what we are after is limit setting in the context of love, and although this sounds simple, it can go wrong in lots of ways. For example, at one end of the spectrum, we can have strict, authoritarian relationships with our children. Here's a summary of that approach, which you can think of as the limit setting without the love:

1. Make rules;
2. Punish when rules are broken;
3. As the children grow older, make new rules;
4. If more rules are broken, make harsher punishments.

It is possible that you will achieve some degree of obedience with this approach. Of course, it will come at the cost of the parent-child relationship, which is bad enough. But even worse — even, in other words, if you imagined that you were willing to sacrifice your relationship with your child to teach values — you won't even do *that* successfully. Because what the child will learn is to avoid detection. Without the context of love, your children will not internalize and come to own the values you are seeking to teach. In the end, then, you will both lose your relationship with your child *and* fail to teach the lessons you felt were important. Harsh, authoritarian parents are feared, rejected, and, in the long run, ignored. And on the off chance that their input *is* internalized, the odds are their children themselves turn out to be rigid, authoritarian jerks.

At the other end of the spectrum, there are parents who set no limits at all. But in the name of "openness of communication" or "fostering creativity" or any of a host of other trendy sounding ideas, children end up with too much power. You can see the result of this approach in many ways, for example in young children allowed to run amok in restaurants or other public venues, with parents benignly looking on. Or in older children who exhibit open defiance to parents who fear their anger. Once again, these systems fail at both pragmatic and philosophical levels. That is, the rules themselves are ignored, the household is chaotic, and the children, taught that their own needs are supremely important, are demanding, self-absorbed, narcissistic nitwits. But at a deeper level, this approach betrays a fundamental misunderstanding of development. Through the years, children have all kinds of thoughts and urges, some of them kind and sympathetic, but some of them aggressive and selfish. Learning to delay gratification — that you simply can't always get what you want when you want it — is one of the most important things we teach children. It's a hard lesson for some children to learn, and it can only be taught through clear and consistent limits.

Parents who don't set any limits at all do damage in other ways as well. For example, as a parent, you may have forgotten that the fantasy life of a child can be a very scary realm. The monsters under the bed feel real in the dark, and nightmares invade your sleep. It's good to know that the grownups in your life are in charge and can make those monsters leave you alone. In later years, teenagers fight tooth and nail against limits. But at a deep level, most of them both want and need limits. In the struggle to figure out who they are and what they believe, they need to push against something. If we back off, they'll just keep pushing until we finally take a stand. But by that time, we may have allowed a whole host of behaviors that we never intended to sanction. Without attempting to address the sociology of the matter, it's my opinion that the inability to set limits on children (and on teenagers in particular) is the signature failure of the baby boomer and millennial generation of parents. Today's parents seem almost afraid of the anger of their children, which in turn gives those children power for which they are not prepared. It is the natural state of things for teenagers and parents to be at odds over rules. Teenagers think they are ready to navigate all phases of their lives. We think they are high-powered speedboats, skimming across the surface of life with no rudder and no chart. There *should* be conflict, which will naturally devolve from time to time into arguments. But if rules and consequences are handled consistently, openly, and without anger (at least on the part of the parent), this conflict does not need to lead to long-term relationship damage.

Punishers

That's enough philosophy. Let's get back to practical matters and look at some specific aspects of using punishers. First and foremost, punishers work best when they are short term and immediate. Short term means that they are over as soon as possible. Immediate means that they fall as quickly as possible on the heels of the behavior. If you punish your child on Friday for what he did on Monday, it won't work. He won't be up in his room regretting what he did five days ago — he'll just be angry. Another example: as parents of difficult children, we frequently get calls from school about our child's behavior in class. I am sympathetic with the plight of teachers, and supportive of their efforts to manage behavior in their classrooms. But it is not good behavioral practice to punish a child at home in the afternoon for behavior that took place hours before in a different location. It's not immediate enough. It doesn't work. Likewise, taking away a privilege or a prized object for a single night works better than taking it away for a week. "Is it short term?" and "Is it immediate?" are the questions you should always ask yourself when you are designing punishers for any behavioral plan.

There will be some further discussion on the topic of choosing reinforcers and punishers, but I do want to specifically mention the most used punisher in the behavioral repertoire:

time-out. The term "time-out" refers to the technique of separating the child from the current situation by sending them to a specific location, usually to their own room, or to a spot designated for that purpose which is away from the main flow of the family. Virtually everyone who talks about behavioral interventions talks about time-out — and for good reason. It is relatively easy to apply, relatively mild, and, if used properly, meets the criteria of "short term and immediate." As part of a clear and predictable behavior plan for children who are old enough to tolerate being essentially alone, time-out can serve many useful purposes. It gives the child time to calm down. It gives the parent time to calm down. It states, without lecturing, that the child is not going to get what she wants by breaking a rule. Keep it relatively short (about as many minutes as the child is years old), don't get drawn into emotional discussions, and let the child reenter the scene when time-out is over. You can use the child's own room, a stairwell, a chair removed from the action, or any other convenient location. If your child seems not to care or even to enjoy the time in her room, so what? We just want her to cut out the problematic behavior, not to make her suffer. If, as can happen, you have the kind of challenging child who flat out refuses to go to time-out, then you have a different sort of problem. You are in the big league. We'll get to that later.

On a side note, while we're dealing with punishers, I often get asked about spanking as a form of punishment. Leaving out the social, cultural, and legal aspects of the question, let's have a look at spanking (or any other form of physical punishment) purely as a behavioral intervention. As a method

21

for engendering behavior change, there may be situations in which it is moderately effective. However, almost invariably, there are very undesirable side effects, including most particularly sadness and anger. In addition, it is virtually impossible to eliminate emotion from the interaction (on the part of either party), which, as I have noted above, raises the level of complexity exponentially and detracts from the intended behavioral goal of the intervention. Dispassionate spanking? Not likely. In addition, are we not frequently trying to teach our kids that violence is not a viable form of communication? And what happens, by the way, when your child is fifteen years old, as big as you, and hits you back? I've had the ill fortune to watch that scene play out in my office, and I can assure you that it's not a pretty sight. Whatever you may have heard by way of the classic "spare the rod and spoil the child" arguments, physical punishments are too much bang for not enough buck. Become a better behavior manager. You won't need to hit your child to get results.

Reinforcers

Returning to basic behavioral principles, the other major method to alter behavior, as noted above, is with reinforcers. Specifically, a reinforcer is a stimulus that, when applied after a behavior, increases the likelihood of that behavior being repeated. Punishers work best, as you recall, when they are short term and immediate. Reinforcers, in contrast, can be less immediate and longer term. As with punishers, what constitutes a reinforcer for one child may not be the same as for another. Likewise, what works for a child at one age may cease to work at another. (No one said this was easy.) Choosing reinforcers, therefore, is sometimes a challenge, and we will return to this question in a moment. As with punishers, however, you must think in a disciplined manner when you are trying to understand what is happening in your family: if you applied what you thought would be an effective reinforcer after a behavior, and the rate of the behavior didn't increase, then either you didn't find a reinforcer or there's something else in play (e.g., a less obvious reinforcer or punisher).

Now if we, as parents, accept that reinforcers and punishers are going to be our tools, then the remaining questions are clear:

1. What are the rules (and therefore the target behaviors)?
2. Should we use a reinforcer, a punisher, or both?
3. What should those reinforcers or punishers be?

As simple as those questions seem to be, answering them is not always easy. Let's examine them in order.

Rules

Oddly enough, most families don't know their own rules. Or, to be fair, most families haven't clearly established a set of enforceable rules that they follow with any degree of consistency. So let's start there: if you say you have rules, but you don't consistently enforce them, then you are certainly teaching something, but it's not what you want to teach. You are teaching your children that you don't mean business. Why should they listen to you, if you don't mean business? When I ask parents what their rules are, I might get a variety of answers, some of which might make sense. But when I ask what happens when the rules are broken, I almost always get either embarrassed silence or some tale of inconsistency. Let's be crystal clear: rules without consequences are not rules. They are suggestions. If your children follow all your suggestions, then all is well. You don't need rules. Lucky you. But if that were so, you wouldn't be reading this book. And if you only have suggestions, it doesn't make sense to be upset with your children for not following them. Make consistent rules with consistent consequences. Your home will work better. So, if you're having behavioral problems in your home, the first question to ask is this: what are the rules? The second is its inseparable twin: what are the consequences for breaking the rules?

Of course, this raises the question of what the rules should be, and we'll come to that in a moment. But the first issue to examine in this regard is how to conceptualize the form of governance in a home. The most effective model of governance in a family is a benevolent monarchy, consisting of an equally empowered queen (mother) and king (father), together with much loved and respected (but powerless) peons. We consult our children on the rules and listen to their input regarding reinforcers and punishers, because that is an effective way to get them invested in the success of the system, and because we do not want to come across as dictatorial jerks. And in fact, as the years go by, their input sometimes becomes more useful. However, at the end of the day, *we* make the rules, *we* establish the consequences, and *we* follow through. With young children, these rules may revolve around hitting or picking up toys or going to bed. Later, they will certainly involve cars and phones and drinking and all the complexities of the teenage years. By this time, I assure you, you will not want to have taught your children that you don't mean business, or that the king can be played off against the queen. Get it right when they're young, and the teen years are a lot easier.

Now back to the rules themselves, and the questions of what they should be about (i.e., what, in behavioral terms, are the target behaviors), and how they should be structured. Rules, first and foremost, must refer to clear and observable behaviors. "You must hang up your jacket when you come in the door" is a good example. No one is confused about the definition, and it's easy to see if it was done. "You may not hit your brother" is another example of a viable rule. However, "you need to have a better attitude" does not work, nor does "you need to try harder." The targets are impossible to define and impossible to measure. "Clean up your room every Saturday" *sounds* good, but it's problematic in several ways. What, specifically, does "clean up" mean? To whose standards? And by what time? Saturday, after all, goes until midnight, does it not? Smart children are pint-sized lawyers, and flaws in a rule system are our problem, not theirs. "By noon on Saturday, you need to have this list of things done in your room" is a much better rule. And by the way, if your child finds a hole in your rule system, don't get angry. Plug the hole and move along. Rules function best when they are clearly defined and tied to clearly defined consequences, both of which are known to all in advance. All rules are negotiable. (Except, of course, after they've been broken. Then it's too late.) If you no longer need a rule, get rid of it. ("Useless rules weaken necessary rules" to paraphrase Montesquieu.) If your child convinces you that a rule is not fair, then change it. If you make a stupid rule that doesn't work, apologize and get rid of it. You are, after all, the benevolent monarch and have unlimited power to admit mistakes.

It follows from the same reasoning that you can't make rules about things you can't measure or can't control. We will return to this idea in context, but briefly, you can make a rule that your child must get into bed and turn the lights off, but not that he must go to sleep. You can make a rule that your child may not curse or shout at you, but not that he cannot be angry at you. You can make a rule that your child must sit at the table, but not that he must eat. And to deal directly with a topic that often comes up: you can make a rule that your child must *act* with reasonable respect, but not a rule that your child must respect you. At the end of the day, our children will respect us or they won't. If we know our own values, act accordingly in our own lives, and run our families consistently and in accordance with those values, then by and large they'll end up respecting us. We can check with them when they're twenty-five to find out. At fifteen, they'll be mad at us from time to time. They'll say we're ruining their lives, and that we are remnants of an earlier age, and that no other parent is as strict as we are. So be it. We'll talk about this more when we get to the teenage years.

Let's admit it: most rule systems fail because of parents, not because of children. We have poorly defined rules with poorly thought-out consequences, which we apply inconsistently. It takes time, effort, and coordination between the adults in the home to design and implement an effective rule system. For single parents, or parents with fundamental disagreements about what the rules should be, it's even harder. However, every minute you spend at this task pays off a hundredfold when your child is older and the stakes are higher. If you don't follow through about clean rooms and bedtimes and rudeness and the million little things that arise with younger children, then why should your children take you seriously about drugs and alcohol and sex? Nine times out of ten, when a parent tells me that his "children don't listen to him," it is because he has, unintentionally, trained them not to. (It's probably ten times out of ten, but I'm trying to be nice.)

Reinforcers versus Punishers: How to Choose

Punishers (and time-out) lend themselves best to more acute and immediate behaviors, and direct transgressions of rules. As noted above, when you make a rule, you need to attach a punisher, so that handling the misbehavior is calm and consistent. Break the rule? Get the consequence. Simple.

Reinforcers, on the other hand, are useful for longer term and less acute problems. Let's suppose, for example, you have an anxious child who is having trouble sleeping in her own room at night. Certainly, we would not want to punish her for being

Adrift in the Digital Age
•

fearful. However, we could design a system that kept track on a calendar of the nights she was able to stay in her room and allowed her to work toward a desired goal. If she sleeps a certain number of nights in her room, she gets the reinforcer. This way, we're incentivizing the behavior we want, without implying that she's somehow "bad" because she's anxious or afraid. It also makes sense at times to combine reinforcement with rules and punishers. For example, you can have a rule against hitting (and, of course, an attached consequence), combined with a reinforcement system keyed to "violence-free days," which, again, get counted on a calendar.

The problem of what to choose as a reinforcer or punisher is more complex than it sounds. Sometimes, the answer is obvious. If your kid wants to wear shorts on a winter day when you think it's not a good idea, don't fight it. If his knees get cold, that's a natural punisher. If his teacher doesn't let him go out to recess, that's a natural punisher, too. But most often, we must come up with a consequence that is relatively unrelated to the target behavior. Your starting point is to observe what your child does for fun and remove access to that thing for some period of time. The electronic world, for all its complexity, has helped us in this arena. It's easy to design a punisher consisting of short-term and immediate removal of a cell phone or a video game. As we noted above, time-out is a useful all-purpose punisher that lends itself well to short-term and immediate application. You just need to be creative and patient, and you'll find something that works. Do not, by the way, pay any attention to your child saying to you that he "doesn't care" that you sent him to time-out or took away his game. If common sense tells you that he does care, then you are probably right. Saying "I don't care" is most frequently an attempt by your child to draw you into a discussion and reclaim a degree of power in the situation. Just remember that our goal is not to torture him, it's to get him to cut out the problematic behavior. If he cuts it out, then in truth, we don't care whether he "cared" about the punisher. Sometimes, you can simply ask your child what would work as a punisher. If he plays a part in the design of the rule system, he may be more likely to be invested in its success.

Reinforcers can also be designed with the help of the child, so that you are certain she is working toward a desired goal. But again, a simple alternative plan is to observe what your child does for fun when she's left alone and allow more time for that. Over the years, I've seen many different reinforcers used with success, from Pogs (remember them?) and Pokémon cards (at the moment, back in fashion), to milkshakes and hamburgers. From a behavioral standpoint, it doesn't much matter what you choose as a reinforcer, as long as your child is motivated to work for it. It's amazing what children will do for a sticker on a calendar. In addition, unlike punishers, you can stretch out reinforcement schedules (i.e., have it take longer to get to the goal), which works well for longer-term behavioral goals. For example, you can note on a calendar a behavioral success, and when the child has put together five successes, she can cash them in for the reinforcer.

Of course, plenty of behavioral situations present themselves for which we may not have designed specific rules in advance.

In those situations, it's most effective when the punishment fits the crime. You threw a toy across the room? You lost the toy for the evening. The toy broke? Oh well. Throw it away. You acted like a brat before you were supposed to go to a party? You don't go to the party. Natural consequences are, in short, the best — but only if they are short term and immediate. When no natural consequence presents itself in an unanticipated situation, we may simply have to let the moment go, step back, and take the time to work out a new rule and corresponding consequence. There's no harm in saying to a child, "Well, we clearly need a punishment for that, but I don't know exactly what it should be right now, so I'll have to think about it." In the meantime, he can worry. We like that.

To be fair, we should acknowledge that there are times when it's almost impossible to do good, consistent behavior management. Here are three of them: 1) in the morning, before school (because of the time limitations); 2) when you're in the car driving; and 3) when you're shopping. There's no real solution to this. You just have to anticipate the problems you have in these situations, and try the best you can to allow for them in advance. It won't be perfect.

And now a final note on the importance of consistency. It's a bit counterintuitive, but it's sometimes worse to have rules that you enforce inconsistently than to have no rules at all. Think of it this way: if you've ever been inside a casino, you have certainly seen the slot machines in use. We all know that if you play the slot machines, you will eventually lose money. And yet, people play them for hours. In fact, this may be the only activity where people will spend a hundred dollars to make fifty and feel like a winner. Why is this? What you are seeing at work here is the power of what is called a "variable ratio schedule of reinforcement." (Stick with me. You'll see how this applies to parenting in a second.) Let's say you hit a winner on your fifth try. When will your next winner come? There's no way to know. It could be your next try. Or maybe five more. Or fifteen, followed by seven and then by twenty. This intermittent reinforcement has a powerful impact on human behavior, and in fact maintains the behavior of sticking in tokens even in defiance of the logical observation that, in the long run, you are certain to lose money.

Now think of, for example, a whiny child. None of us wants to teach our children to whine. However, how many of us have, after multiple requests to stop fussing, finally given in to a fussy child "just to get him to quiet down." Consider what we have taught that child: a little whining may not be enough to get what you want — but hang in there — if you are obnoxious enough, you'll finally get your way. You may need to whine just a little, or this time it may take some truly dramatic whining. In other words, like a human slot machine, we have taught our child that persistent bad behavior will ultimately have a payout, so don't give up easily. The conclusion: don't give in to whining or, with older children, to eye rolling or tears or anger or any other attempts to subvert a rule system that is in place. Teach your children that reasonable rules will be consistently enforced, and that they will *never* get what they want by confrontation or defiance or whining.

To summarize what we've said so far:

1. Have as few rules in your family as you need;
2. Choose target behaviors that are clear and observable;
3. Determine the consequences of breaking a rule in advance and, whenever possible, discuss them with your children;
4. Apply the consequences (punishers) in a matter-of-fact manner, with as little emotion as possible;
5. Make your punishers short term and immediate;
6. For longer term and less acute behavioral issues, consider using reinforcers instead of punishers;
7. Be consistent.

Now, let's move on to issues that arise as the years move along.

The Early Years
Sleep, Food, Tantrums, and Defiance

Start with the basic idea that any behavioral planning we do for young children should fit into the overall context of conveying to the child that the world is a reasonably safe and reliable place to be. This has always been the central task of the early stages of parenting, and the arrival of the digital age has not changed a thing. Although we can't *prove* that "self-esteem issues" and "anger issues" and other problems that emerge later are directly linked to early childhood experiences, it seems reasonable to assume that these years are important at a very foundational level. This is not to deny the heavy hand of nature in the "nature–nurture" debate. On the contrary, I've always suspected that whoever it was who speculated that children come into this world a "blank slate" only had one child, because no one who has more than one doesn't know that children are different from day one. Nevertheless, a predictable and loving environment undoubtedly provides the most fertile soil for the benign and healthy emergence of whatever seeds genetics may have sown.

This does not mean, however, that there is no relevant application of behavioral principles, even at these early ages. Let's examine, for example, the issue of crying. Clearly, an infant doesn't have many ways of communicating, and crying is a legitimate way of saying anything from "I'm hungry" to "I'm sick." However, crying is also a behavior, and an annoying one at that, so as time goes on, we want a child to use words to express needs, as opposed to crying. So here is the dilemma: if we don't provide a young child what he needs when crying is his only way to ask for it, we teach him that the world is unreliable and arbitrary. But if we continue through the years to give the child exactly what he seeks every time he cries, we are reinforcing crying. (And, of course, if we are inconsistent, then we are slot machines, and teach the child that if he cries long and loud, we will ultimately give in.) There is no perfect solution to this dilemma. Sometimes you'll decide that the crying is a behavioral artifact and isn't expressing a real need, and you'll ignore it. Sometimes you'll decide that there's a real problem, and you'll answer the call. At age one, you'll usually respond. At age six, you'll ignore more often. Sometimes you'll be wrong. But if you spend enough time with your child, you'll develop a sense for when something is *really* amiss, and you'll be right most of the time, which is the best that any of us can do.

The issue of putting a child to bed provides an excellent example of this sort of problem area. Here's the question: should you let a child cry herself to sleep, or should you go in and try to calm her down? There's a school of thought that says you should just let her cry. She'll learn that no one is coming (i.e., that the crying behavior is not going to be reinforced), and she will ultimately "self soothe" and fall asleep. Personally, this approach always seemed a bit heartless to me. The idea that we would be right there meeting her needs during the day, and then abandon her to the tender mercies of the monsters that lurk in the dark of night, just never made sense to me. I understand the theory that crying is a behavior that we do not want to reinforce. However, the fears of a child are very real to her, and it is a strange lesson to teach her that we are right there, hear that she is afraid, and are not coming. In addition, it simply doesn't always work. My oldest son, an energetic and determined lad, after being fed, sung to, gently tucked in, and abandoned, was capable of screaming with such violence that he would throw up. Whereupon he would have to be calmed, bathed, re-fed, and re-put to bed. We gave up the idea of letting him "cry himself to sleep." However, if I'm going to be totally honest, the truth is that just letting them cry themselves to sleep sometimes works. So there's probably nothing wrong with trying it. Choose a specific amount of time, and allow your child to attempt to get to sleep on her own for that time, even if there's crying. If it doesn't work, either lie down with her or sit next to her crib until she falls asleep. Then sneak out of the room, without waking her. Good luck with that. (I hope you don't have a squeaky floor.)

The moral of the story is this: there is no one-size-fits-all solution for this kind of dilemma. Some children will separate easily from their parents, fall asleep, and sleep through the night. Others will cry for a few minutes, fall asleep, and be fine. And others will present a more substantial challenge. One of the

35

best-kept secrets of parenting is the number of families with children who sleep in their parents' bedroom. The fact that this seems odd to us is, it seems to me, the real oddity. After all, for most of human history, parents and children have slept in the same space. It is a very modern notion indeed that even the youngest children have their own, separate, lonely sleeping space. If your (somewhat older) child is having problems sleeping in her room, put a sleeping bag on the floor next to your bed, and tell her not to wake you up when she comes in. But in any case, you have to find a solution that works for you, and it may not always be what you would do in a perfect world. After all, you need to get some sleep yourself.

While we are on this topic, let's address the question of when a child should *stop* sleeping in his parents' room. The answer: when he's ready. I understand that when parents ask me this question, this is not the answer they want to hear. However, we cannot require a child to stop being afraid, and we certainly don't want him to stop coming to us because he is more afraid of our anger than he is of the demons that haunt his nighttime imagination. Never punish a child for seeking you out in the night. Remember that the line between dream and reality is not as clear for them as it is for us, and they are truly frightened. With older children, use a reinforcer system that keeps track of and rewards nights during which the child doesn't come into your room. Be patient, and allow sleeping separately from you to be an accomplishment that your child owns. In the meantime, just relax and let your child come in when he needs to. On balance, you'll probably get more sleep than if you lug him back to his own bed and try over and over to get him to stay there. None of this will do much for your sex life — but then, you have young children, so all the spontaneity is gone in that department anyway.

Tantrums

A child who is having a true tantrum is not in control of her behavior. Think of it as a circuit overload. Nothing useful is going in. There is nothing to be taught or learned during a true tantrum. Just wait it out, and don't let the child hurt herself or anyone else. Don't reward it, and don't punish it. Don't waste your time trying to figure out if it's "real" or "manipulative." To the extent that it is a behavioral issue, what you teach by not responding is that a tantrum will not work as a form of communication. To the extent that it is an inarticulate expression of frustration, you can just keep the child safe, let the tantrum run its course, and move along. Some children rarely have tantrums. Some have them all the time. This probably has more to do with neurology than anything you've done as a parent. Tired children are more likely to tantrum, as are hungry children. Get them to bed earlier. Feed them. Sensitive children respond poorly to unpredictability and changes in routine, so if that's the case try to be as consistent in your routines as possible. However, if you have a tightly wound child, you're going to deal with tantrums from time to time, no matter what you do. Don't beat yourself up, and don't get angry at your child. After all, we don't get to choose our neurology, and if we did, we wouldn't choose to be sensitive or tightly wound. (And anyway, as I will remind you from time to time, your child got that neurology from you or your spouse.) Clueless people in grocery stores will give you that look that implies that you are doing something wrong and they could do better. You're not, and they couldn't.

While we are on the topic of young children, I'll just state the obvious: you never want to set up a behavioral system or a rule that you can't enforce. This is true at all ages, but is sometimes less apparent with young children. As we have noted above, you cannot, for example, force a child at any age to eat, sleep, or eliminate. Yet generations of well-intentioned parents still *try* to do it, which is why we need to have a look at the topic. A quick review: you can say, "You have to sit at the table while the family is eating." You cannot say, "You have to eat." You can say, "You have to go to bed." You cannot say, "You have to go to sleep." And you can say, "You have to sit on the toilet." You cannot say, "You have to go." These may sound like meaningless semantic differences, but they are not. Even at an early age, your child is gaining a sense of control and autonomy, and this is something you want, both in the short and the long term. There are plenty of situations in which we will give our children no options, but we will choose those situations carefully, they will be battles worth fighting, and they will be battles we are certain to win. The three examples above do not represent that kind of battle. On the contrary, application of punishment systems around these topics is a mistake, and can lay the foundation for the kind of power struggles between parent and child that are frustrating and exhausting. Ultimately, your child will eat, sleep, and poop. Offer reasonable options and be patient. When your child *chooses* to comply in these areas of self-management, it is an achievement and we move along. When you *force* compliance, even if you succeed at that moment, you just set the stage for another battle on another day. We will return to this question when we reach the topic of school attendance.

Food

Food is a particularly difficult subject, so we will examine it while we are discussing young children, although it can come up at any age. For various reasons far too complex to address here, food has become a tremendously ambivalent topic in many of today's societies. During most of the history of humanity, it was likely not an issue. When you are required to cultivate and gather and hunt your food, obesity is rarely a problem. When your meat either runs away from you or fights back, there's rarely too much of it. (And what you do acquire is lean, from all that fighting and running.) At those times, people could simply follow their instincts: eat whatever was available until hunger was satisfied. There are some lucky people in first world countries who can still get away with that approach. They are either active enough or have high enough metabolic levels to burn all the calories they eat; they gain weight as they grow and plateau when they have matured. But for most of us — and particularly as we grow older — this is not the case. We simply cannot follow our instincts. We cannot eat whatever we want in whatever quantities we want, or we get fat. And in many cases, the same is true of our children.

As you will have noticed, this presents parents with a paradox. On the one hand, we cannot force our children to eat (let alone, to only eat "healthy" foods). On the other, we cannot simply allow them to eat whatever they want. The best approach lies in the tactic of "stimulus control," which in this situation is the behavioral name for providing options, but limiting the choice to food items we can tolerate. You inform yourself sufficiently about nutrition to have a variety of healthy (or at least not unhealthy) choices available, and you don't be overly concerned about which option your child chooses.

Here's how it might work. Let's suppose it's important to you that your family eats meals together, so you are all sitting at the table. However, one child doesn't want to eat what is being served. Now, there could be any number of issues at play here, from the simple (he doesn't like the taste) to the complex (control, anger, etc.). However, as an experienced, calm behaviorist, you know that you don't have to understand the underlying issues. (And you certainly don't need to make an emergency call to your child psychologist.) Just have a simple, reasonably healthy "go to" second option (like a bowl of cereal with milk). No need for discussions, lectures, anger, guilt, or any of the rest of the drama that can accompany mealtime. There is certainly no need to cook an entirely different meal for a picky eater (a practice, by the way, that runs the risk of empowering resistant behavior, which you don't want). If there's a dessert involved, it's reasonable to make it dependent on eating the healthy parts of the main meal, as in, "No, you don't have to eat your vegetables, but no, you can't have dessert if you don't." As parents, it's part of our job to do our best to provide healthy meals that our kids like. But we don't need to be giving nutrition lectures to three-year-olds, we don't need to be in power struggles over food, and we don't need to lose sleep over our children having Cheerios for supper. Not a big deal.

Children who eat too much present a different problem. Again, the underlying forces at work can be simple or complex. And again, our best plan is calm and thoughtful stimulus control. If you keep bags of chips and candy around your house, do not expect your children to choose carrots as a snack. The fact that *you* have learned as an adult to limit your consumption of junk food is of no help to your child, who cannot. Get the junk out of the house while your child is growing up. It's a better plan than having a locked Twinkie cabinet. (I didn't make that one up, by the way. I worked with a family that had one.)

As the years go on, you may also have to apply the concept of stimulus control to vulnerable times of the day as well. If your child gets home from school at 2:30, and the adults are not home until five or six, there is an uncontrolled window of opportunity that many children can't handle. You may need to find an after-school program or location, so that your child is not presented with too many unhealthy options. It is disheartening to listen to a conversation between an angry parent and her overweight child about the child's inability to control her food intake. Everyone feels horrible. If your child can't handle a food situation at some point in her life, work at changing the situation.

41

Regarding food, what you are seeking is control, without being controlling. This is an important distinction, and you will hear it both explicitly and implicitly throughout this book. *Control* means that we have rules about what a child can and cannot *do*. *Controlling* means we try to have rules about what a child can and cannot *feel*. The former is simply limit setting, and it is a critical element of parenting. The latter is fraught with guilt, anger, and all the other elements of the pattern that poisons relationships within a family. The former is easily understood by a child. The latter gets embroiled with self-esteem issues, depression, and myriad other complex psychological phenomena. You don't want to go there.

Overt Defiance

As noted above, some children are openly defiant. Sometimes this is in part our fault: we have unintentionally taught them that if they resist long enough, they will get what they want. However, sometimes we just have a tough kid. If you have one of these, don't despair — but fasten your seat belt for a complex ride. Again, it's useful to start by attending to all the obvious external factors, such as food and sleep, which can make an edgy child even more volatile. Keeping his world as predictable as possible can also help, as these children often respond poorly to unexpected changes in the rhythms of daily life. Keep a family calendar in an open and accessible place, and refer to it often. Start talking about transitions well in advance (the start of school, for example), and move the family patterns toward what they will be in advance of the actual transition.

But there's only so much you can do, and if you have a tightly wound kid, there will be problems. Let's start with a basic point: you do not want to let your child's moods run the home. If you let her get away with unacceptable behavior because you don't want to "rock the boat" or because you're afraid she'll "lose it" if you confront her, then you may get by that moment, but you will pay the price in the long run. The family will end up tiptoeing around her moods, and she will gain a sort of power and control that is not healthy for her and not healthy for you. I am sympathetic with sensitive or volatile kids. They didn't ask for this irritable neurology. However, they need rules and limits, just as all children do. Unfortunately for you, it takes more effort, patience, and expertise to manage these kids than it does for their more docile siblings. You need to be more clear and specific about your rules. You need to be more consistent. You need to be even more certain to keep your anger out of the equation. And, predictably, each of these aspects of the process is more difficult. Especially the anger part.

Let's look at an example. Suppose you have a nice clear rule, the accompanying punisher for which is time-out. Now suppose that your child breaks the rule. Calmly and immediately, you point out that he broke the rule, and you send him to time-out. So far so good. But at this point, he screams "no" and runs away. (Clearly, he has not read the behavior management handbook.) Do you chase him? Do you shout at him? Do you physically force him into the designated time-out location? Do you give in, and live to fight another day? Do you call in the cavalry, and get your spouse to handle it?

Well, no, no, no, no, and no. Why not?

1. If you chase him, he has dictated the course of the action. The event is no longer about the target behavior, but about anger and fear and control. And what if you can't catch him? And what do you plan to do if you do catch him? Tie him up?
2. If you shout, then this is all about anger and the relationship, not about the behavior in question. We've discussed this. It doesn't work.
3. Using physical force is a dead-end street. Maybe you can dispassionately carry a three-year-old to a time-out location without escalating the problem. Maybe. But a seven-year-old? Unlikely. What if he hits you? What if he just gets up and runs away again?
4. Never give in. Never. If you do, you will be teaching your child that you can't control him, which is scary for him and depressing for you. If you can't control him at age three, what is your plan for when he's fifteen?
5. This is tricky. It's the classic "wait 'til your father comes home" approach, and its flaws are less obvious but just as damaging. For this one, let's look at an example:

I once worked with a couple who had an extraordinarily difficult child. For a variety of (irrelevant) reasons, his father was better able to manage his behavior than his mother. But instead of working at being more effective herself, the mom simply called for help whenever there were problems. If the dad was at work, she called him on the phone. If he was elsewhere in the home, she shouted for him. You can guess where this led. Although this approach was occasionally successful at getting by difficult moments, the child heard the message that his mom couldn't control him by herself, and as a result his behavior was far worse with her than with his dad. This left her feeling incompetent as a mother, her spouse feeling that he was always the bad guy, and the child himself — a perceptive little dude — feeling guilty that he created tension between his parents.

So what *should* you do with open defiance? The answer, as you would expect, lies in the same realm as it always does: calm, dispassionate, relentless enforcement of the rules. In the scenario described above, the child *will* ultimately go to time-out. If she runs away, she'll come back. Nothing else is happening in her life until she has done the time. What do you do yourself? Read a magazine. Wash the dishes. Disengage. When she tries to pull you back into a verbal battle, you simply point out that she needs to do the time-out before you are discussing anything with her. If this takes an hour, so be it. It might take the whole evening. Doesn't matter. Because, in addition to applying the punisher for the original misbehavior, this is now also about you being calm, reasonable, and in charge. And you are making this statement both to your child and yourself. Have faith that, in spite of her resistance, this is what your child both wants and needs. If you do this when she's young, you maximize her ability to internalize her limits, which will in turn maximize her ability, in the longer run, to manage her own behavior.

Of course, this may not happen any time soon. And, as your child battles against giving back any power he may have already acquired in the family, matters may get worse before they get better. Sorry. That's why parents frequently give up at this point and just take the easy way out of the moment. But if you do that, you have taught your child that, ultimately, he is in control. And you are not. As we move into the school years, that's not a lesson we want our kids to have learned.

School Anxiety

Well, you've made it through the first few years, and the prospect of school is looming. Should be easy, right? Drop her off, and enjoy all that free time. The internet isn't much of an issue with kids this young, so no particular worries there. Maybe you'll be able to go back to work yourself and get back on track in your career. Simple.

Except when it isn't. I'm not taking a position here on whether children are more anxious now than in the past. I don't know. Maybe we're just paying more attention. Either way, anxiety problems are extraordinarily common, and unfortunately they often wait for these times of transition to greet us with unexpected challenges and dilemmas. For example, here's one: how insistent should you be that your child goes to school, even if he's anxious about going? If you are facing this problem, you can rest assured that you're not alone. It's complex, deeply disruptive to a family — and common.

As we have noted in other contexts, we could speculate at length about the underlying causes. We could talk about social anxiety, separation anxiety, pressure for achievement, and a variety of other issues, any of which might have validity in your situation, and all of which are worth a look. If you're having difficulty stepping back from your own case and making an objective analysis of the forces at play, this is one of those situations in which consulting with a psychologist can be useful. However, whatever the underlying issues may be, the behavioral analysis is likely to be straightforward and something like this: 1) going to school provokes anxiety; 2) staying home relieves anxiety; 3) a repeated pattern of getting ready for school (provoking the anxiety) and then staying home (relieving the anxiety) forms a powerful learning paradigm and quickly becomes entrenched, resulting in the behavior called "school phobia." We'll discuss this pattern in greater detail below, but that's the basic picture. And it can present, unfortunately, at virtually any age, from preschool through high school.

If you find yourself in this situation, the first thing to examine is your own attitude. You probably have an anxious child on your hands, and you've probably always known it. If we are talking about a young child, maybe she's sensitive to noise or to crowds. Maybe she cries easily and has always been sensitive emotionally. At any rate, you've probably always protected her to some extent from the chaos of the world. And now you're supposed to abandon her, crying inconsolably, to that very chaos, trusting a stranger to fill your role. It doesn't feel right.

Let's make a couple of points, still referring to younger children. First, if you are at all ambivalent about dropping him off at school, he'll know it. The thing that sensitive, emotional children do best is read our emotions. If *you* get upset when *he* gets upset, then your emotions become a part of the behavioral paradigm. You do not want to be rewarding him (relieving his anxiety by taking him home) for missing you. Before you start the school process, get it clear in your head that your child is, within reason, developmentally, socially, and intellectually ready to go to school. Accept that his going to school is one of the first steps in the long and intricate process of his becoming a strong, autonomous person — separate from you. There is, I grant you, an odd irony in the fact that we spend the first four or five years of a child's life protecting him from all the sharp edges of life, and then just drop him off into a world which we know is full of edges, trusting in the skill and sensitivity of strangers. But the social skills and defenses necessary to survive in that world are the product of exposure to it, and you do your child no favors by pretending otherwise. Be at peace with the process. Your child is more resilient than you think.

In short, the first step in addressing the problem of a child who is having a difficult time attending school is with your clear, consistent, calm message that she *will* end up going to school. If not now, then in fifteen minutes. If not this morning, then this afternoon. If not today, then tomorrow. For the vast majority of children, this is enough. Don't worry if there is some clinging and crying (as long as it's not coming from you). Teachers are used to this. Make the drop-off as quick and matter-of-fact as possible, and get out of there, because you are a dependency stimulus, and you will get in the way of her adjustment. Go home, take a walk, and trust in the virtually unlimited capacity of the human brain to adjust.

But what if it doesn't work? What if you have a child who truly falls apart and can't recover? These are tough situations, but let's start by saying that everything we noted above still applies. He needs to go to school. However, there are children for whom it is predictable that separation will be a problem, and, as we noted above, if you have one of these extremely sensitive little guys, you knew it a long time ago. The arrival of school does not mark the first time he's fallen apart. It happened when you got a babysitter. It happened when you tried day care. It may even be happening every night when you try to put him to sleep (more on that later). Often useful in these situations is a variant of a technique called "systematic desensitization," which simply refers to gradual exposure to the feared stimulus. In this case, it means that long before the first day of school, you take him over to the school building and get him used to the place. Walk into the building. Find a time when his teacher is there, and introduce him. Show him where the bathroom is. Back at home, run through the routine of getting ready for and going to school in the weeks before school starts. What you are doing is removing the power to cause anxiety from as many of the elements of the situation as you can, long before the actual first day, so that the day itself isn't such a radical change of routine. Get your spouse to do it without you as well, so that it is less about parting from you personally and more about adjusting to the school routine. Get the school on board, if you need to, so that someone who understands your situation meets you for the first few days and whisks your child away.

I can't overemphasize the importance of your own attitude as a parent in the arena of school anxiety — and this is critical regardless of the age of the child involved. You must not convey to your child, by thought, word, or deed, that there is an alternative to going to school. Regardless of how sympathetic (not to mention agonized) you feel at her obvious distress, you must be clear in how you handle yourself that she *will* end up going to school. There is no Plan B. The trick is to be sympathetic about the fact that it is hard, without implying that there is a choice. As is true of anxiety in other contexts, school anxiety is not a subject that non-anxious people understand very well. As parents, we try to sort out the line between what a child *can't* do from what she *won't* do. The problem is that the child herself may not know where the line is. But the harder you push, with the assumption that your child could do this if she wanted, the more she will need to prove to you that she can't. Avoid the power struggle. Admit to yourself that you can't really know how difficult this is for her. Recognize that you will not achieve the results you want by dragging her to school, because she will not own the decision and thereby own the conquest of anxiety. But do not back down from the ultimate reality of school attendance. Home schooling for philosophical reasons is an entirely separate issue. Home schooling as a treatment for school anxiety is a mistake at any age, because it reinforces dysfunctional

51

behavior. Anxious people don't become less anxious by avoiding anxiety-provoking situations. Write that down.

Now let's have a more specific look at how school anxiety manifests at later ages. As you would expect, this is a difficult and complex topic as well. We'll come back to this issue later when we deal with computer gaming, but basically older children and teenagers often don't simply say, "I don't want to go to school." Instead, they can't get out of bed. They have headaches, stomachaches, and all manner of other symptoms. You suspect there is school anxiety involved, but how can you be sure there aren't real medical issues going on as well? The fact is, you can't. And no one wants to be the iron-fisted hard case parent that forced his child out the door, only to have him throw up on the bus. So, of course, you go to your pediatrician and rule out medical concerns.

But what if nothing shows up medically? Or what if this is the third time around, with vague, ill-defined symptoms? What you do not want to do is launch into debate mode with your child about whether the symptoms are "real" or "all in her head." You will get nowhere by telling someone who says that they are in pain that they are not; this is simply not an approach that will lead to any sort of useful discussion. On the contrary, the angriest and most resistant adolescents I see in my office are those to whom it has been implied — often by both physicians and parents — that their pain is not real. At the same time, not unlike the approach you take with younger children, you cannot let the idea take root that there is, in the medium or long term, an alternative to going to school. Not to be repetitive, but just like with younger children, if she can't go this morning, she goes this afternoon. If she can't go today, she goes tomorrow.

Let's now, as I promised above, take a closer look at the learning paradigm involved, because a look at the underlying dynamic will explain why this attitude and this approach are so important. Start with the premise that your child, for whatever reason, feels anxious about going to school. When the decision is made, either by him or by you that he doesn't have to go, he feels immediate relief. This relief is a powerful reinforcer, and it "teaches" the child that school avoidance will lead to good feelings. All the elegant, rational lectures we may give concerning why this is a bad idea (how will he *ever* be a nuclear physicist?) are not as powerful as the relief from anxiety, right here and right now. And here's what will make you even crazier: in the afternoon (after missing school) or at night (with school still hours away), you will have a "good talk" with your child and think you have gotten through to him. He may even lay his school clothes out and remind you to get him up. But in the morning, he will pull the covers up over his head and turn over. Or he will have the "worst headache he's ever had." And he must stay home. What parent could be so cruel as to send such a suffering victim to school? And, of course, when he stays home, he misses class and falls behind, which in turn increases the anxiety about going back. Not to mention that he sets himself apart socially ("where were you yesterday?" his friends ask), which does the same. If all of this is combined with a symptom (such as headaches), which is by no means unusual, then you have the inevitable doctor visits and clinic appointments and trips to specialists as well. All of which involve missing school.

School personnel are stuck as well. If they take the "tough" approach, they may increase the anxiety surrounding going to school. But if they back off by decreasing assignments or providing in-home services, they may enable the behavioral aspects of staying home. One school recently told a student I was working with that she "didn't have to worry about the homework." Obviously, this was a benign attempt to decrease the stress for her. But telling an anxious person not to worry is about as successful as telling her not to breathe. Anxious people worry. This student worried that she was falling further behind and was angry at the school for not providing her with the means to keep up.

And if that weren't enough, there's a cognitive component, too: your child starts the invisible but insidious process of saying to himself that he "can't" go to school. And once he has said to himself that he "can't," then what's the point of trying? And why should he listen to the parade of parents, teachers, shrinks, and other possibly well-intentioned but certainly ignorant adults who don't understand that he can't? So he walls himself off from everyone who is trying to help him, because they just don't understand, and they make him feel that the whole thing is his fault, or that he is faking the symptom, or that he simply isn't trying hard enough.

There is no simple solution here. Parents (both!), schools, the child himself, and any other support personnel involved all need to be on the same page with respect to how to handle both the time at school and the time at home. Maybe there's a resource room he can retreat to when he feels anxious. Maybe there's an adjustment that can be made to the material he has missed. At the very least, you will ensure if your child does stay home that he has no access to TV, the internet, gaming, etc. But whatever the specifics are, they need to be grounded first in the steady, relentless, unemotional assumption that there *will* be a return to school, and second in the steadfast refusal to enter into an angry power struggle. This can be an extraordinarily difficult balance to strike and, as we noted, deeply disruptive to a family. But I can tell you this: over the years, I've worked with families who simply, at some point, gave up and let their child stay home. Not a one of them, in later years, is glad they did. And neither, truth be told, are the kids.

Homework

As long as we're on the topic of school, let's talk a little about homework. Getting your kids to do their homework is often a pain. But it's important. Not because the work itself is important. Sometimes it is, but most of the time it isn't, if we're going to be honest. Which is why we have those annoying conversations in which our children indignantly declare they shouldn't have to do their homework, because they're never going to *use* whatever it is they happen to be studying at the moment. Here's your answer: homework is part of the job of being a student. It's a lousy job, of course. Bad pay, and bad hours. (Good vacations, though.) But it's their job at this time

55

of their lives, and they don't get to choose. Later, they'll have choices, but not now. And truthfully, later, they'll have bosses who give them work they don't like, but that they'll have to finish. Say this: "In this family, we do our jobs, and we do them well. And we don't complain." One of the great things about being a parent is that you get to define your family values and make them stick. That's why you can start sentences with "In this family . . . ." Getting your children to do all the homework every night is how you help them build good work habits, and it's well worth spending the time to do it when they're young. They'll certainly need those habits when they're older.

How much external structure you will need to execute this task depends on how much internal structure your child has. If she's naturally organized, it won't take much. Lucky you. If she's not, you'll need to help. We're not, however, going to spend time on the specifics of how to help here. I just googled "how to help your child do homework" and got 224,000,000 hits, so I think the topic has been covered. But no matter what you decide to do, keep a couple of things in mind. If your child is having a hard time at school, you can expect her to resist doing homework. No one wants to come home after a day of feeling stupid and incompetent at a job and feel stupid and incompetent at home. Expect effort, not perfection. Also, if your home is chaotic and inconsistent, that won't help. Tighten up your own act, and you'll be helping out your child at the same time. Most of all, don't get angry. Not wanting to do homework is the natural state of a child, not a moral issue. Be relentless but be patient.

Self-Esteem

Self-esteem is the sort of topic on which everyone agrees in a vague way. It's good to have it, and bad not to have it. However, what "it" really is, in concrete terms, is harder to define. And if you can't define it, how do you go about fixing it or, for that matter, fostering it in the first place? For our practical purposes here, let's think of self-esteem as "what a person says to himself about himself." Although this sounds simplistic, it's a useful formulation, with far-reaching and complex implications, because now we can examine how someone comes to the point of saying things about themselves internally. Take for example the descriptor "lazy." If, for whatever reason, we regularly call a child lazy, then this can become the child's internal description of himself. And if I believe I am lazy — if that is how I describe myself to myself — then why would I be motivated to try hard at anything? After all, no one expects me to. Including me.

As the parent in that scenario, what we intended to do when we called our child lazy was to (mildly) punish him. We assumed he would not like the description and would respond with redoubled effort. But we forget that a child's concept of himself can be very fragile indeed. You only fight back with redoubled effort if, inside yourself, you are certain that you are *not* lazy, and you want to prove this to the person who called you lazy. Without that certainty, you are vulnerable to simply accepting the "lazy" diagnosis, internalizing it, and owning it. You don't fight back because you believe, deep within yourself, that you may in fact be lazy. I have been with many teenagers who have reported to me, in a resigned and fatalistic way, that they were lazy, as though this were a defining and immutable aspect of their personality. It does not cross their minds that they can simply do their homework and the descriptor will no longer apply.

Schools and teachers are frequently unintentional co-conspirators in this process of forming a distorted internal monolog within a child. For example, we know that certain types of learning are more difficult for certain children than they should be, given their overall aptitude. In other words, some smart kids don't do as well in school as it seems they should. That, in simplest terms, is the definition of a "learning disability." Sometimes these kids can't do the times tables. Sometimes they don't read very well. Sometimes they are disorganized and can't focus. Early in the game, they figure out that school is a tough and unrewarding place for them to be. And most important, early in the game, they figure out that trying harder doesn't result in better performance. Teachers, drawn from the population that did well in school, frequently just don't understand these kids. For them, working hard made sense, because when they worked harder, they did better. Therefore, it makes no sense to them that a student wouldn't simply try harder, if she were having problems. In the context of self-esteem as we have defined it above, school helped these teachers form a solid foundation. The internal monolog for those teachers went like this: "when I work hard, I improve." The world of school seems fundamentally just and fair, if the deal is that when you work harder, you do better.

But what happens to kids for whom that simply isn't true? What if, when you work harder, you *don't* do better? What if you work harder, don't do better, and get called "lazy" or a "classic underachiever" or a "dimmer bulb" or any of the countless mildly scornful descriptions I've heard over the years from teachers in faculty meetings? I cannot tell you how many times I've heard teachers say, "He could easily be an A student, if he'd just try." Let me state this: if your child seems bright enough to "easily" get A's, but he is doing poorly, there's probably something going on from a technical learning perspective. That he is simply lazy is the least likely explanation.

And what if, as the student in the scenario, your teachers believe this nonsense about you, and convey this to your parents, who also start to look at you in the same vaguely disappointed way? It's no wonder that so many kids with learning problems are either angry or sad (or both). To be clear, a central truth in the lives of children with attentional issues and learning issues (or "disabilities" or "differences" or whatever they may be called this week) is that when they try harder in school, they don't necessarily do better. So why *should* they

59

try? I recall once giving a pep talk to a young learning-disabled man named Josh about doing his homework and trying harder. He looked at me mournfully and said, "You don't get it." I asked him what I didn't get. He said, "If I don't try at all, I get a D–. But if I work my ass off, I get a D. So what's the point?"

This is not to denigrate the efforts of special educators, the parents of kids with learning issues, or teachers in general. However, often in our efforts to focus on the material to be learned, we lose track of the internal life of the child — of her self-esteem. I care a lot less whether my child can recite the times tables than I do that she feels like she's stupid, that she'll never succeed in school, or worse yet that she's a disappointment, hates learning, and will never succeed in life. As adults, we all have seen many examples of people who were unsuccessful in school, but who have gone on to be just fine in life. (Just as we have seen examples of excellent students who were lost in the real world.) As a child, you do not see this. What you see is three major forums for success: grades, sports, and physical attractiveness. If you do not feel successful in any of these areas, then what is your basis for self-esteem? Or, to phrase the question behaviorally, if no one else is saying good things about you (except perhaps your parents, who secretly wish you *were* doing as well as their neighbor's kid and whose opinions don't really count anyway), then why would you say good things about yourself in your head? As an aside, it's amusing to watch well-intentioned but clueless adults try to address this issue through sports. Certainly, you can give every kid who shows up a trophy, and you can pretend every game ends in a tie. But it won't matter. You don't fool the kids. They know who won. They know who was the star. And they know who wasn't. The roots of self-esteem lie deeper than telling everyone that they are "special."

I'd like to momentarily return to Josh, because he illustrates another problem: we adults frequently fail to sufficiently recognize the critical importance of just simply trying hard. His parents and school were looking for grades, not effort. He was in fact, from his perspective, punished for working hard — or at the very least not reinforced. But resilience (which we may define as bouncing back from failure) combined with the willingness to work hard are probably more predictive of long-term success than raw skill. You'll do your child a favor by focusing on these attributes as opposed to obsessing about grades.

Here's the central point I'm making: as parents, we have a major voice in defining success. If we were really hoping for the class president, the captain of the football team, or the valedictorian, and are disappointed that all we got was a normal, nice kid, who works hard but is "only" a B student, then our children will know it and will feel that they don't measure up in our eyes. I once sat with a fifteen-year-old girl who had two high-achieving siblings and said this to me: "My brother is my mother's favorite. My sister is my father's favorite. I'm no one's favorite." She was a normal, nice kid, a solid student with a big heart and plenty of empathy, but none of the flashy skills that get you into fancy colleges. And she felt like a total worthless failure: in her words, "ugly, fat, and stupid." Another young woman told me once that she "hates those days at school when they give out prizes — there's just nothing special about me."

In the long run, we need to help our children understand that being a good person is far more important than getting good grades or being coordinated, and that nothing is more trivial than being pretty or wealthy. (Living in a culture that worships athletes and cute rich people is perhaps not much help in this endeavor.) However, in the short term, this is not much solace to a child who feels stupid, awkward, and ugly. Self-esteem, then, if it is the product of anything, is the product of success. Part of our job as parents is to provide as many forums as possible in which our children can find that success. As we noted above, sports and grades are there for everyone, but they don't work for everyone. Therefore, you should be open to trying anything within reason in which your child shows interest: music, dance, drama, art, martial arts, horseback riding, and scouts are just a few examples of less standard outlets. I recently had a young man inform me that his parents had bought him a forge, and he was excited about trying out swordsmithing. Good idea. Why not?

In short, it is indeed helpful from the standpoint of building self-esteem to be on the lookout for arenas in which your children can be successful on their own merits. If you find something, if they succeed, and if you value that success, then that will help. Redefining success, as we have noted above, also helps. At the end of the day, however, low self-esteem is sometimes not a fixable problem in the short term. Your child may go through a time when she feels horrible about herself. (I might venture to say that most thoughtful and introspective kids go through such a phase.) Telling them that they don't need to feel that way, or encouraging them to think of all the great stuff in their lives, or reminding them how many people are worse off than they are does not work. In fact, it's counter-productive, because you are telling them that they shouldn't feel what they feel — or worse, that they should feel guilty for feeling it. Sometimes, you just stick with your child during this period. Not to sound too much like a psychologist here, but be patient, be supportive, acknowledge and accept the feelings (even when they don't make logical sense to you), don't get angry, and don't let yourself get pushed away. Feeling lousy about oneself as a teenager is hard to go through and hard to watch. But it's good for building the ability to be empathic. How else does one develop the ability to understand and support others who feel lousy about themselves?

While we're on the topic of self-esteem, there's one final group of kids I want to mention. One of the unspoken truths about parenting — a fact we often don't admit to ourselves — is that some of our children are, in fact, harder to love than others. The neurology of some children, for example, makes them sensitive, volatile, and temperamental. They may cry easily. They may be picky eaters. They may be easily distracted and hard to please. They may have difficulty learning and get into trouble at school. And yet these children have the same need to be loved and valued as their more docile and cooperative siblings. Their self-esteem is just as critical to their success and just as dependent on the love and acceptance of their parents. They didn't ask for their spiky neurology. Yes, they are annoying. No, you can't get angry at them for the way in which they are wired. You, after all, gave them the wiring. If you cannot accept them as they are, love them, and help them adjust to and cope with a world in which they are an imperfect fit, then who will?

Bullying

Bullying is inevitable. Wherever there are power differentials and insecure, aggressive people acquire power, that power will be abused. This is true regardless of the continuum of power in question. Big people bully smaller people. More popular people bully less popular people. Older people bully younger people, and so forth. Since schools by their nature house all these continua (and many more), there will always be bullying in schools.

Let's pause for a moment to briefly address the institutional question of bullying in schools. Why am I doing this in a book aimed at parents? Because you have a right to know what to expect of your child's school and a right to advocate for your child in this regard. There should not be a single teacher or coach or administrator who fails to understand the vulnerability of the school environment to be fertile ground for bullying. Nevertheless, attention to this issue is sporadic at best. It is only in the wake of tragedy — a suicide by a bullied child, for example — that major focus is brought to bear on bullying. And for some amount of time following such events, we see seminars and focus groups and guest speakers and workshops and "anti-bullying" protocols. And then the interest dies down until the next crisis.

Here is the point I am making: in an environment as conducive to bullying as a school, intervention must be systemic, ongoing, and proactive. Everyone with direct student contact must, by word but especially by example, address this issue every year. Each year, a new version of the power hierarchy emerges, and the abused become the abusers. It is never going away. Teachers, coaches, and others who remain silent, perhaps comforting themselves with some version of the notion that "that which does not kill us makes us stronger," should remember that Nietzsche was not a developmental psychologist, and his philosophy is cold comfort to a frightened, bullied child. Sometimes that which does not kill us beats us down, reshapes our inner lives into wastelands of anger, sadness, and discouragement, and makes us feel powerless to effect meaningful change. I will agree that overprotective, helicoptering parents who attempt to cushion their children from the tiniest bumps of life leave those same children ill-prepared and lacking in resilience. I will not agree that educators should stand back from the entirely predictable nexus of damaging behavior created by bullying. The world at large will provide our children with plenty of examples of cruelty and injustice, to which they will need to adapt. We don't need our schools to do it.

Bullying
•

However, as always in this book, our primary purpose is not to argue philosophy (or to engender institutional change), but rather to figure out what to say and do when a child comes home in tears because he was picked on at school. So let's get to it. As is so often the case, the parental response to this problem exists at more than one level: 1) you want the bullying to stop; 2) you want to armor your child such that he is more resilient and less vulnerable to being bullied in the first place; and 3) you want to do all this in a way that doesn't turn your own child into a bully if, at some future date, he acquires power. The answer to number three lies in the way you handle numbers one and two, so let's look at them all together.

It goes without saying that you will be angry at the child who bullied your child and probably at that child's parents as well. You will want to fix the problem, using the power you have accrued as an adult. But this is not about you, and neither your anger nor your impulsive retaliation will meet your goals. Getting bullied is painful, but it doesn't have to be cataclysmic, and your child is watching you to calibrate her own response. Your response, then, should be supportive, but not excessively angry or sad. As we noted above, all schools have bullies, and navigating the world of school is part of the life of any child. Listen to her story from start to finish, without letting your own feelings get in the way. Whether spoken or unspoken, your message is this: "I'm sorry this happened to you, and I understand how you feel." At a deeper level, your message is that bullying says a lot more about the bully than it does about the victim, but putting that directly into words probably won't help much. It's too philosophical. Bullying is

67

an assault on self-esteem. Your plan is to shore up that self-esteem by your assurance, in both word and attitude, that your child can handle the situation and that the actions of trivial people will not change the opinions of important people. Keeping your own anger out of the picture is how you guard against your child's internalization or expression of that anger, which in turn guards against your own child turning into a bully down the road.

Along those lines, here's a quick story: I was once talking to a group of ninth graders, who were complaining that the privileges granted to twelfth graders at their school amounted to institutional bullying and intimidation. I told them I wasn't certain that they would be able to change the system in time to help them as freshmen, but that I was absolutely certain that they could change it for freshmen of future classes. They asked how. I said, "When you are seniors, abolish the privileges." "No way," they said. "If we have to put up with this, so can they." So it goes. Bullying can breed new bullies, crush the spirit, or be a part (albeit a painful part) of the growth process. That's why you need to think through how you handle it.

Let's now return to the practical steps you may decide to take to make the bullying stop. In many cases, your actual courses of action may be limited, and some actions may make matters worse for your child. They may mark him as a tattletale. They may provoke revenge, whether on the bus or on the playground or some other time when the teacher isn't looking. That's why whatever you decide to do should be discussed with your child. Remember that he already feels disenfranchised and powerless in the situation, and the last thing we want to do is inadvertently victimize him a second time. Do you contact the parents of the bully? That depends on your judgment of them and your relationship with them. Some parents are helpful and responsive. Most, unfortunately, get defensive at the notion that their child is a bully. Sometimes, to be fair, you may find that your own child did not give a completely unbiased and dispassionate description of the events in question. In other words, the answer to this question is: it depends.

Do you contact the school? Once again, there's no easy answer. Schools and individual teachers vary widely in their skills at handling these issues and in ensuring that the victim does not get scapegoated. Certainly, contact with the school or teacher should be a consideration, as they have from a practical perspective the widest range of options for intervention that minimize the risk of pinning the blame for the intervention on your child. It is also possible to just ask the school to keep an eye on the situation, without taking immediate action. In milder cases, you may, with your child, decide to do nothing, and see how things go. Your child may feel enough stronger, now that he "knows that you know," that he can handle the situation. And be sure not to allow even low-level bullying to take place over extended periods of time; that's what leads to the kind of depression and hopelessness that in turn leads to tragedies. Be prepared to take action if the situation worsens, and think through what you will do, if that happens. In all cases, take your own child's unique situation into account: age, support network, resilience, self-confidence, etc. Tailor what you decide to do to his style and his needs. Keep in mind that this isn't about following a formula. It's about what's best for your child.

Let's now turn to the topic of cyberbullying, the toxic digital offspring of bullying in general. As we are all aware, teens can be remorselessly cruel to each other. However, the indirect nature of social media has unleashed unprecedented levels of additional casual cruelty. And if that weren't bad enough, the meanest kid at school can follow your child up to her bedroom and torture her all night long. This is why, and I'll say this repeatedly, you need to monitor your child's use of social media closely during these years — to the extent that you allow it at all. If you find that there is some degree of online bullying going on, you'll ask yourself the same questions as above: Do you contact the school? Do you contact the parents? And there are others: Do you take your child's phone / tablet / computer? Do you block access to social media? At the very least, you will continue with your policy of keeping internet-enabled devices out of your child's room at night. (You have that policy, right?) We'll discuss these issues further when we get to the chapter on electronics.

In more serious cases of bullying, or in any case where there is an element of physical assault, you take immediate action. Specifically, do you encourage your child to hit back? Clearly, there are widely varied opinions on this matter, involving religious beliefs, your child's own personality, and so forth. I think it's pretty difficult to tell a child he can't defend himself, but I leave this question to the parents. In any case, we do not

70

let our child get beat up, even if he is desperately afraid that our intervention will make things worse. We do not let him get repeatedly humiliated. We listen to and respect our child's opinions and requests on these matters, and we involve him in the decision-making process. However, we are in charge of protecting him, and there is a line past which we must not allow matters to go. Certainly, it's an arbitrary line — but you'll know it when you see it. And when you do, put your carefully considered plan into action. Maybe talk to the school. Maybe talk to the parent. Certainly, take action.

Electronics, Social Media, and the Internet

There is no way to anticipate what may have changed in the world of electronics between the time I write this and the time you read it. One thing is certain: the landscape will continue to change, and will continue to present parenting challenges. And the minute you have a plan for the present, the future will render your plan obsolete. As a parent, you cannot escape this; there's nowhere to hide. But once again, all is not lost. There are principles that can provide guidance and direction, and you will be able to translate them to your situation, whatever that may be. Let's have a look.

First and foremost, you cannot parent today without at least a working knowledge of the digital world. For better *and* for worse, it is here to stay. The first "digital natives," people who grew up surrounded by electronic devices, were born in the nineties, so the contingent of completely clueless parents is steadily dropping. Nevertheless, there are still plenty of parents around who are not digitally literate, so let me repeat myself: you cannot responsibly raise a child in the twenty-first century without a knowledge of computers, smart phones, the internet, social media, and whatever else ultimately presents itself. You don't have to love this stuff. You don't even have to use it. But you do have to understand it, along with its risks and rewards. If you are reading this as a parent and you are not comfortable in these areas, get busy. Take a course. Sit down with a friend. Open experimental accounts on all the social media platforms, even if you cancel them in a month. Surf the internet through the eyes of a young person who has more curiosity than caution. Explore the topics that most interest young people, and don't neglect the ones that frighten you — drugs and sex and anorexia and cutting and depression and anything else you can think of. Look at the images. Look at the videos. You will, if you have not already done this, be horrified to find out how easy it is to end up in some very dark places. When you imagine your ten-year-old child sitting up in his room doing this by himself, you will take your role as gatekeeper to this world more seriously.

Electronic Devices

Let's start by looking at rule systems for electronic devices that don't access the internet. In this case, you will have some decisions to make about their use, but they will be relatively straightforward and will include such questions as: How many hours of use is healthy? When is a video game too violent? When and how does homework fit in? What time do the devices go off at night? These questions are not unlike those we've always had to ask regarding, for example, television. Which is not to say that they're easy or unimportant, because electronic entertainment is well-designed, compelling, and can easily become an obsession for a child. If you say, for example, "You can have screen time when your homework is done," you have in one sense incentivized finishing homework. Which is good. But at the same time, you have incentivized *finishing* homework, regardless of the quality. Which is not good. A better plan is to decide how much screen entertainment you think is healthy for a school child to have on a school night, and schedule it in. You also have the option of simply saying "no" to screen entertainment during the evenings before school. Your children will moan, of course. But there is little doubt that video games and their ilk compete with reading for non-homework hours. And equally little doubt that reading is better for brain development. By the way, and we will note this again regarding internet-connected devices, do not expect your children to turn off these devices by themselves, once they are in bed. Collect them at bedtime.

In general, I find common sense more helpful than the research literature with all of these decisions. If some form of electronic entertainment seems too violent, it probably is. Watching a road runner whack a coyote with an anvil probably won't spawn a serial killer. Bloody scenes of decapitation and mayhem, on the other hand, are probably not a good idea for a young child. The use of games to occupy children on long car rides or to allow parents a couple of minutes of extra sleep on a Saturday morning is probably fine. Hour upon hour glued to the screen on a beautiful summer day is probably not. Why not? It's too passive, too asocial, and builds habits that will need to be broken later. It competes with other activities, especially reading, that are better for cognitive development. Kids with attentional issues tend to get hyper-focused on video games, and breaking them away is a pain for everyone involved. Socially anxious children substitute virtual relationships for real ones, which means they don't confront their anxieties in a productive way.

What you are doing here is stating that you, as parents, will decide the amount of time available for electronic entertainment and how it will be regulated in the service of health and family values. It is worthwhile to remind yourself that the people who designed and sold you your hardware and software are not in the parenting business. They are in the sales business. They are not your allies. You will have to make these decisions based on your beliefs and on your ongoing observation of the impact of these devices on your children. Expect to have to make rules. Expect your children to resist those rules. Why should this part of parenting be different from any other? And now on to the heart of the matter: the internet.

The Internet

Devices with access to the internet are another question entirely and one you cannot avoid. Schools, for example, are constantly expanding their use of the internet, even in the primary grades. Which makes sense, as the internet offers access to virtually unlimited resources, together with historically unparalleled ability to individualize both the pace and focus of learning. However, the door to all of this is also, regrettably, the door to the sewer.

Your job as a parent is to make available the positive resources while shielding your child from the (to put it mildly) inappropriate content. Even the most well-intentioned child can misspell a web address or search term, or click an innocent looking ad banner, and end up in a dark corner of the web. So the first thing you need to look at is which devices access the web and how they do it. This book is about getting the philosophy right, not about instruction in technology, but here is the briefest primer, for those who need it. Access to the web comes basically in two ways: through WiFi (either in your home, at school, or the various places where public WiFi is offered) and through cellular data. Some devices can only access the web through WiFi (e.g., some tablets), and others can do either (e.g., your smart phone). If you are going to control access to the web, you must handle both situations. WiFi in your home comes through your router; thus, you can set up web filtering on your router, which will ensure that every device in your home has restricted access when connected to WiFi. You can also, these days, selectively turn off or pause access to the internet for specific devices through the router. In addition, each web-enabled device used by your children should be equipped with restrictions, because they will use them in places other than your home. How to do all this? Just google, for example, "how to filter the web on a browser," or "how to childproof the internet," or "how to childproof a laptop," or similar terms. I did this while I was writing this paragraph and found dozens of straightforward guides to the technology and applications currently available. As systems evolve, this information will evolve as well. Some of you will find this easy. Others will not. However, as we noted above and will repeat later, you cannot simply look the other way and hope for the best. If you are reading this book, you take parenting seriously. Every serious parent needs to do this.

Here's why this is so hard: because we are still in the relatively early stages of the prevalence of the internet, we have no common wisdom or past practice to guide us. When you take a stand with your children on access to the internet, you may feel you have very few allies out there. This is because you, in fact, have very few allies out there. Many parents have simply abdicated their responsibilities in a way that would be unimaginable if it had to do with drugs or sex or driving. They don't understand the internet or the devices very well, so they provide them to their children with very little oversight. After all, they reason, *every* kid has a smart phone now. Why not mine? Schools, for their part, have insisted on internet access for homework, without adequate help for parents in managing the broader implications of web access. Again, let's use some common sense here: you should assume that you will need to set limits. You should assume that your children will resist those limits. You will need rules and consequences. You will need to expend time and effort to follow up on those rules. In other words, this is another area of parenting where the tools of behavior management must be put to work.

Now, let's get more detailed with some of the decisions you will have to make regarding internet-enabled devices, remembering that, as in all areas of behavior management, the ultimate goal here is not our ability to control our children's behavior, but their ability to control themselves. The specific ages you choose to allow access, and the degree of limits and controls that you impose on that access, are necessarily arbitrary. However, this process should be arbitrary in a thoughtful way, based on your own values and your knowledge of your child. You control more when they are younger. You back off the control when they show they can handle the responsibility. The internet has snuck in under the radar of parenting because the consequences of its misuse are often less visible than those in other areas. But less visible does not mean less important.

As we have noted, a point will arrive in a child's schooling when restricting all access to the internet is not practical. Productive use of the internet in schools is exploding, and this will only become more prevalent in the future. However, let's get one thing clear: no child in the primary grades should have unrestricted access to the internet. Not on a computer. Not on a smart phone. Not on a tablet. On the other hand, by the time they are juniors and seniors in high school, there is no further point in restrictions. They are getting ready to leave your home, and the internet is a fact of life. It follows logically that the years from ages twelve to sixteen are the time during which the systematic introduction of the internet takes place. So how should you do it?

Let's start with the question of cell phones. Because of the rapid move from the introduction of cell phones to the prevalence of smart phones (with access to the internet), the lines here have become blurred. From a developmental perspective, a child's readiness to handle a cell phone and the same child's readiness to handle access to the internet are unlikely to occur at the same age. Why, then, are we handing our children smart phones as their first device? Why are we giving access to social media to children who have not shown that they can handle access to texting? Here is what I would suggest: make a cell phone available to a child when it is helpful for you, as a parent, to be able to establish pickup times and address other logistical issues with your child. Roughly speaking, many children at age ten or eleven can handle this. Keep in mind that when you do this, you need to address a variety of attendant issues. For example, to whom is it ok for your child to give his number? What are appropriate times to call? How does phone use fit in with homework? Are there family times, where phone use is not allowed? (Do not hesitate to designate times — meals, for example — when the family is simply together without distractions, and keep devices away from these events. Including yours.) Does the phone go to the child's bedroom at night, or does it stay under parental control? What sorts of things is your child allowed and not allowed to say in texts? In the early years, you should not allow any deleting of texts, and you should check the phone often (daily at the start) to ensure appropriate use. Today's children (not to mention today's adults) need to learn the critical lesson that anything produced in digital form can live on forever and is infinitely replicable. They need to learn that they never want to send a text that they wouldn't want their parents — or the parents of the person to whom they sent it — to see. When you read their texts, your children will moan that you are "invading their privacy." You will tell them that, regarding these devices, they have no rights of privacy. The digital world is not private. Period. At the start, program in their contacts: that's whom they have permission to call and text. No one else. And if your child cannot handle any of these strictures, then she is not yet ready for access to a phone. Take it away. Put it off for another three months, or six months, or whatever you decide. To summarize: your child must prove to you that she can handle calling and texting responsibly before you let her anywhere near social media and the internet. You will check that use every day at the start, and you will take the phone away at the slightest hint of irresponsibility. And if you decide to use a smart phone with internet restrictions instead of a simple cell phone, you better be certain your child doesn't know how to get around those restrictions.

Smart phones and other devices with access to the internet represent an entirely different can of worms and pose an entirely new set of questions. Those of you who are familiar with the technology will know what these questions concern: innumerable (and constantly evolving) platforms for communication (e.g., Facebook, Instagram, Snapchat, etc.), gaming (including online and offline versions), photographic sharing (of the benevolent and less benevolent varieties), virtually unlimited forms of video entertainment, countless apps, and, of course, complete access to the rest of the internet. Each of these is, in its own way, a tool that can be used in a beneficial way.

And each can be misused. The same application that allows your son to arrange a spontaneous pickup soccer game also allows, as we have said, the meanest kid in his class to follow him home and harass him in his bedroom. The same application that allows your daughter to share her vacation photos with her cousin allows her to send a nude picture of herself to a "friend" who then shares it with every child in her class. The same internet, so critical for a history research paper, also allows access to websites extolling the virtues of religious fanaticism, anorexia, or bomb making. And if you think I am overstating the case, then I must tell you that you are naïve. Access to these devices, as well as to all others that offer connection to the internet, should be allowed in a controlled, systematic, and tightly managed manner. And, as I have mentioned, neither your school nor the parents of your children's friends, most of whom studiously ignore these issues, are likely to be of much help to you.

There are no hard-and-fast guidelines governing the pace and timing of the rules you will enact. Much will depend on the maturity and stability displayed by your children. Even more will depend on the central family values that you bring to the table in all aspects of your parenting. As noted above, when your children are in sixth grade, they are not ready for unlimited access. When they are juniors or seniors, they had better be ready, because they are about to be out on their own. Therefore, ages twelve to sixteen are, as in so many other areas, the sweet spot for tough parenting decisions. Just like drinking. Just like driving. Just like sex. Interesting years. We'll get to that other stuff.

As far as specific rules for the initial introduction of these devices, I have, as you might expect, some suggestions:

1. Control the times at which your child has access to the devices. Set aside homework time in the afternoon or evening, and take the devices away during that time.
2. Put a bowl in the kitchen, and that's where the phone goes at homework time. Same thing at least a half hour before bedtime.
3. As noted earlier, put parental controls on all devices and on your router.
4. Enact rules of politeness regarding phone use. Follow them yourself.
5. Maintain total parental access. No passwords that you do not know. No deletions. As a parent of a young teen, you must insist on (and use) complete access to all digital communication by and to your child. All texts. All tweets. All posts. All emails. All social media. Everything. Your child will hate it. Too bad. This is how you both protect them and teach them appropriate use. You would not, with no restrictions, hand them the keys to a car. You would not, with no guidance, allow unrestricted access to alcohol or drugs and trust that your fourteen-year-old will use good judgment. Don't do it with the internet.

These are absolute minimum rules. Start with them, and add more, if you need them. And, of course, remove them, as you no longer need them. Make use of the emerging technology (e.g., "Circle," from Disney) that lets you individually control the devices in your home, and turn them off at appropriate hours — always remembering that devices with cellular data are not confined to using WiFi. But make no mistake: as fast as these new applications come out, your children will find ways around them. There is no substitute for physical control of the devices themselves.

What if the rules are broken? Take the device away, or back up to an earlier and more restrictive version of the rule in question. For example, in the case of a simple infraction, like forgetting to leave the phone in the kitchen when going to bed, the consequence will be equally simple: loss of the phone for twenty-four hours. This meets the criteria of being a short-term and immediate punisher, and has the added advantage of neatly fitting the crime. In the case of more complex or serious infractions (e.g., drug- or sex-related communications), you may decide that your child just isn't yet ready for that level of access, and back up to an earlier level of control (which can last for weeks or, in some cases, even months). In both cases (as in all behavioral interventions), you will want to discuss these potential consequences in advance, when you discuss the rules. Your child will still be angry when it happens. Too bad. If you stay focused on the fact that you are simply doing what you said you would do, you will be able to control your own anger. What if your child tells you that you are "ruining her life," that "no other parent is as strict as you," and that she "hates" you? Well, I feel sorry for you, of course. That stuff is hard to hear. But if you don't hear it at some point about some topic, you're probably not doing your job. And on this topic, since so few parents are doing their jobs, you will be an outlier, even if you make mild rules. You'll take some heat. You can handle it. We'll return to this topic in a moment.

Let's go back briefly and summarize a few key points, because it's important always to keep our long-term goal in sight. We want to keep our children safe, but at the same time we want them to learn self-control in the context of the myriad options provided by the electronic world. The only way to do this is to allow, over the teen years, steadily increasing access, with steadily decreasing parental control, and therefore steadily increasing opportunity to make mistakes. All of which is no different from the dilemmas we face regarding drugs, sex, driving, and all the other arenas that give us nightmares. I have often heard it said that the move to a digital world is "different" from other parenting challenges and that the array of principles and approaches applicable in other areas do not apply. I disagree. What has happened is that parenting has been outgunned by the pace of change. As we noted above, there is no common wisdom guiding us, because the options haven't been around long enough, and they have changed so rapidly. None of this, however, lets us off the hook. There are still plenty of things we *do* know that can help guide us. No ten-year-old should have access to pornography. No twelve-year-old should be taking the sniping of the meanest kid in her class to her room with her when she goes to bed. No fourteen-year-old (or not many) can be trusted to simply shut down his devices and go to sleep at night. We don't need research studies to figure this stuff out.

Just as in all the other complex areas of parenting during these years, you will need to have clear rules, clear consequences, and consistent enforcement. It is true that when you do this, your children will be stunned. That's because, as we've said, many parents aren't formulating and enforcing any rules at all regarding electronic devices in general, and smart phones in particular. On the contrary, we seem, as a society, to be shaping our norms to the use of the phone, rather than our use of the phone to the dictates of courtesy and common sense. And if adults are not establishing those norms, how can we expect it of our children? Young teens don't understand appropriate boundaries (a topic to which I will return in a moment when we look more closely at social media). They post and share wildly inappropriate material about themselves, and then agonize in anticipation of the responses of their peers, while breathlessly commenting on the equally inappropriate musings of those same peers. Certainly, it's easy enough to understand the attraction of social media for young teens. In essence, it's just a juiced-up version of the same world of gossip that has always existed and has always been compelling to teens. As adults, we may do a cost benefit analysis of participation on social media, weighing the advantages of ease of communication with friends against the resultant invasion of privacy. Young teens cannot do this. They do not have the distance and perspective to either maintain their own boundaries or respect those of others. Their obsessive search for validation makes them exquisitely vulnerable, and the internet removes all the restrictions of time and space that used to offer at least some respite from the cruel side of gossip.

It's open season on insecure, lonely children, who are far too early in their developmental arc to protect themselves. That's why we must do it for them.

The topic of boundaries is extraordinarily complex, and I won't explore it in detail here. However, we can't avoid it entirely, if we're going to understand the impact of social media on our teens. In simplest terms, boundaries refer to the limits of closeness that we (consciously or unconsciously) place on our relationships, to keep them healthy. People with rigid boundaries let no one close, and have either no meaningful relationships at all or ones that are shallow and artificial. People with excessively permeable boundaries allow (and expect) inappropriate closeness. They share (and expect you to share) intimate details of their lives, and they may take offense if you don't reciprocate. Relationships with these people are frequently dramatic and volatile; you may in an instant go from being their best friend to their worst enemy.

People with healthy boundaries have a continuum of closeness. They may have a handful of time-tested and trusted friends who sit atop this continuum, others at the other end of the continuum who are clearly not trusted, and a full array of intermediate points of acquaintanceship with varying degrees of intimacy and trust. Healthy boundaries may come naturally to children raised in families where the parents themselves understand the balance between intimacy and intrusion on personal space. (It is for this reason, for example, that I am always on the alert when a teen tells me that her mother is her "best friend." Maybe that's great. Maybe not. Probably not, to tell you the truth.) However, for many children, adolescence is a critical time of growth in this dimension. With self-confidence at a minimum and character development in an early phase, young teens are particularly prone to making poor decisions about what information to share and with whom to share it.

Use of social media comprises a direct assault on boundaries. By its nature, it encourages the publishing of inappropriate content to an inappropriate audience, with the potential for unlimited reproduction to a wider and even more inappropriate audience. As we noted above, young teens are and have always been obsessed with the opinions of their peers. In the pre-smart phone era, parents frequently complained that their teens seemed to care more about what their friends thought about them than they did about family values. But in those days, when a child came home from school and closed the door behind her, she was insulated to some degree from the pressure to conform or be liked or be popular. Now there is no escape. In fact, the needy and insecure internal persona of many young teens is augmented by an equally needy and even more vulnerable online persona, with the brutal and inexorable metric of "likes" and "followers" rendering judgment in real time and around the clock. Little wonder that today's teens seem more anxious and stressed than ever before.

Let me give you two quick examples of how powerful social media has become in the lives of our children. Maria is a sixteen-year-old sophomore in high school. Like most kids her age, she has a Snapchat and an Instagram account. The first thing she does when she wakes up is check her accounts. Then she goes to school, where there are rules about the use of phones. In theory, phones can't be checked more than once a day. But in fact, kids check phones in the bathroom, at their lockers, and wherever else they can get away with it. Teachers are supposed to take phones away that are misused, but no one does. Maria estimates that she gets at least 100 messages per day on a normal school day. On the weekends, she gets "200 or more." She takes her phone to bed with her at night, and is often on it until midnight or later. At any moment, she knows exactly how many pictures she has posted and exactly how many "likes" she has received on the posts. She knows, ranked from highest to lowest, how many "likes" came in on *all* of her posts and from whom. Last year, someone commented on one of her pictures that she had gained some weight. She virtually stopped eating.

Lauren is a fourteen-year-old freshman. She is perceptive, shy, and sensitive. She describes herself as having no friends — but she has social media accounts that she uses daily. Over the summer, she "fell in love" with a boy who promptly broke up with her when school started. Two weeks later, her "friends" talked her into trying to resolve the issues with her ex over social media. She and two of these friends would enter an open chat situation with the boy and two of his friends, all of whom would be able to follow all aspects of the discussion. This was, as you might expect, a disaster. She was embarrassed and humiliated, and the story has been told and retold count-less times. Although she dreads what she will find, she still checks her social media accounts obsessively.

By contrast, let's have a look at Ashley, who is thirteen. She also has Snapchat and Instagram, but generally avoids Instagram, because she doesn't want to deal with the issue of "followers." Ashley was given her first smart phone in sixth grade, but her mother has monitored every phase of its use. She has access to all of Ashley's accounts as well as the phone itself, and she regularly checks it. Most of Ashley's contacts are girls from her dance studio; she has resolved to "avoid the drama" of the social media world. The phone is useful to her, but "no big deal." Ashley thinks her parents "learned a few things" from their experience with her older sister, and she has "just gotten used to" the strictness of the rules.

As we do occasionally in these pages, we're going to take a brief detour into philosophy. I'm stepping back here from the question of specifically what rules to make, because I want to make the case that there are extraordinarily important issues involved here that call for extraordinary vigilance from parents. It's not just that the web and social media provide a constant assault on boundaries. That's bad enough. But far worse in a societal sense is the ability of social media to spread fear and falsehood disguised as knowledge and news. Autocratic governments, of course, embrace this, as it gives them unparalleled power to influence the thought of not only their own citizens, but those of other countries. Representative democracies, caught between the importance of free speech on the one hand and the spreading of lies and disinformation on the other, are screwed.

I have no idea what governments will do about this. As I write this, Congress is scolding the CEOs of Twitter, Facebook, Instagram, and Google. Maybe that will have some impact — we'll see. Governments will struggle with this, and there will political battles about censorship, freedom of expression, and so forth. But I would not wait around for governments to figure this out. Parents can do something right now. But it will take a lot of work, and it will be work that we've never had to do before.

Here's what I mean: not that long ago, when you wanted information that you didn't have, you looked it up. You went to the family encyclopedia. You went to the library. You tried to find an authoritative source. Since there wasn't that much readily available information, it was easy to focus your attention on what you found and try to make sense of it. No one controlled the flow of information, no one followed your progress, and no one profited from your search.

On the internet, however, there are so many sources of information, it's impossible to pay sufficient attention to any of them. In fact, "attention" (in the form, for example, of "clicks" or "views" or "traffic") is manipulated, marketed, tracked, and sold to advertisers. The accuracy of the provided information is hardly an issue compared to its popularity, because the popularity drives advertising revenue. Outrageous, inflammatory content draws more viewers (and more passionate viewers) than sober, balanced debate, and these viewers can be directed to yet more outrageous content, which further polarizes them. And the more people who visit a platform (e.g., Facebook), the more the owners of the platform can charge advertisers, and the more data the company can collect — which is also sold. For our children, finding information is no longer the problem. There's tons of information. But lots of it is false or misleading, and as far as I can tell, very little effort is being made to filter it.

If all of this were just driving our children toward the purchase of a certain brand of phone or pizza, it would be problematic, but not critical. But it isn't. It's driving them toward their position on critical issues, like whom to vote for, whom to blame for their troubles, and, of course, whom to hate. This is not the recipe for calm, thoughtful discussion of complex issues — neither over the dinner table, nor, for that matter, in the Senate. Nude selfies are bad. This is worse.

Here is the bottom line: parents must fully engage with their children's use of social media and the internet as an information source during the early teen years. We must slow down the torrent of input, so that it does not overwhelm our children's ability to make sense of what they are exposed to. We must challenge every assumption. We must train our children to look for the original source of their information, and for the potential motivations and prejudices of the providers of that information. We must help them to realize that even the act of seeking information triggers algorithms which in turn shape (and distort) the information provided. Every "like" and every "retweet" is a piece of data to be collected, sold, and used to influence your child. This is the world we live in. It's a huge additional task for parents and will take tons of effort and time. But it's no one else's job. Therefore, it's ours.

Social Media

With all of this as background, let's get practical and move to the specifics of managing social media. The prime years for the development of secure boundaries and an intact sense of self run approximately from sixth to tenth grade. (Of course, this can start earlier and run for the rest of life, but let's stick with the most common range.) Very few sixth graders have the stability and maturity to handle social media accounts. Neither that which they "share" (a benign word for the dissolution of boundaries) nor what they read from others is likely to be intelligently filtered. If you allow social media at all in seventh or eighth grades, it should be carefully monitored on an ongoing basis. By ninth grade, you essentially can't avoid the issue any longer. Once again, you make rules, monitor, and enforce, and once again you will find that many other parents aren't doing it, because it's hard. We have all seen clueless adults posting boundaryless, inappropriate material, or cruel and thoughtless comments. Why would we expect young teens to do any better? When you monitor, you may find material that generates discussion, which is clearly beneficial. You will find plenty of inane chatter. Fine. Who cares? And you may find a variety of transgressions that call for a variety of restrictive responses. You may find that your child is being bullied. You may find that your child is complicit in

93

bullying someone else. You may find language you don't allow. You may find pictures. Be prepared to terminate access to any portion of the internet or social media that you feel is being misused. Give your kid time to grow up, if you need to.

Additionally, you may find references to drugs or sex or a variety of other themes to which we wish our children weren't exposed. Well, we can wish whatever we want. Our children are exposed, and we must do something about it. There are some parents who take the position that there is no point in making these rules. Kids will find ways around them, they say. That's just the way the world is these days, they say. This comes from the same crowd who brings you such gems as "boys will be boys" to excuse sexual aggression, or "they're going to experiment anyway" to rationalize serving alcohol to minors in their homes. We'll get back to this later, but this is the coward's approach to parenting, expounded by people who either don't care enough, are unwilling to put in the time and effort to do this the right way, or are afraid of the disapproval of their children and their friends. It's our job to stand up for what we think is right, and to make and enforce rules about what we think is wrong. Of *course*, our children can find ways around the rules we set up. Sometimes we'll catch them. Sometimes we won't. But they will always know where we stand, what we believe, and how strongly we believe it. Our rules, calmly and consistently enforced, are the practical manifestation of our values. Our relationships with our children, grounded in love and respect, allow us to leverage these rules into the moral principles that we hope will guide them long after they leave our homes. The electronic world has, to

be sure, presented novel challenges. But it has changed neither our job as a parent nor the critical importance of doing
it well.

Gaming

I want to spend some time here on the topic of gaming, which
is emerging as its own complex conundrum. On the face of it,
gaming is just another relatively harmless form of electronic
entertainment, for which you might need rules and limits. But
it's not that simple. I'm not going to make the case here for the
addictive nature of today's computer games, but if you are not
aware of the issue, spend a little time researching. The fact is,
there is no analog in history for the compelling and absorb-
ing nature of today's internet-based gaming. Here are a few
aspects of what you are dealing with:

1. The games themselves are extremely well designed,
   making maximum use of the video and audio resources
   available, and drawing the gamer deep into their intricate worlds.
2. There is often a built-in aspect of the games that
   rewards quantity of play. The more hours you play, the
   more you are rewarded.
3. Online multiplayer games have a social aspect, in that
   you may be playing (and chatting) with a number of
   others. However, you do not need to be in actual contact with those people. In fact, you don't need to ever
   even meet them — they could be from anywhere in
   the world. Nevertheless, there is the illusion of social

interaction that, for socially anxious people, may in fact remove the motivation to have genuine interactions.

4. The games often have no natural end point. Unlike board games or card games or athletic contests or books, there is no intrinsic time to stop playing. You can game for hours at a time, and you can find people to play with at any hour of the day or night, all without ever leaving your room.

When your child is young, his use of gaming may be quite unremarkable. After all, he is safely in his room, quiet, and fully occupied. In later years, you may comfort yourself with the observation that at least he isn't drinking or smoking weed or having sex. What, you may ask, is the problem?

The problem is not only that what may start as a harmless pastime can become an obsession. By itself, that would be a big enough issue. But there is also the complicated intersection of gaming and anxiety. That is, for socially anxious people, gaming can become a powerful reinforcer. You feel safe. No one can bully you. No one can even see you, so the fact that you may feel unattractive or overweight is irrelevant. You can hide behind your gaming handle or avatar or whatever, and yet not be alone. And the same dynamic I described earlier regarding staying home from school applies here as well: when your anxious child sits down to game, he feels a wave of relief. He is in control. (It will not surprise you to learn that these two problems are frequently combined: children who stay home from school due to anxiety frequently spend the day gaming — a potent formula for developing deeply dysfunctional habits.)

If gaming is so potentially toxic, then why shouldn't parents simply ban it? Once again, the issue is not that simple. Let me make a couple of points to you that have been made to me. By gamers, of course.

1. It is possible for gaming to be a healthy (or at least not unhealthy) pastime in the life of a normally developing child. Why shouldn't someone who has no interest, for example, in sports or music or other more traditional endeavors come home after school and game for relaxation?

2. It isn't just gaming that provides a refuge for socially anxious people. Reading, for example, can be just as compelling and absorb just as much time. And yet if we see our child gaming for hours at a time, we worry. If we see him reading for the same amount of time, we don't.

In other words, gaming (and internet use in general) presents us with a more nuanced set of questions than does substance abuse. Alcohol, for example, is an addictive substance with well-documented toxic impact on the developing brain, and is illegal for use by teenagers. There is no such thing as "healthy" use of alcohol by teens. Gaming, on the other hand, can be harmless, and so must be viewed through the lens of balance. How much is too much? Is it ok on school nights, or should it be confined to weekends? How do you, as a parent, tell when it is taking an unhealthy turn? At what point, in other words, does a relaxing break for a shy child become a toxic obsession that stunts normal social growth and development? Inevitably, as is so often the case, these questions will come down to judgment calls that you will make about your own child. They will probably not be determined by a specific number of hours and minutes, but rather by the role gaming comes to play in the life of your child. However, I must tell you that I have come to believe as a clinician that this is a much larger problem than we have recognized. To get some perspective on both the gaming and the anxiety components of the issue, it may help to step back and listen to some stories, taken from the lives of young men I've seen over the last few years. Let's start with the most extreme case: John.

John

John came to see me at the age of twenty, with a long history of anxiety. By his own description, he was always shy and quiet, and he avoided school whenever possible. As early as first grade, he would fake being sick, get sent to the nurse's office, and arrange for his mother to pick him up and take him home. John says that he thinks both his parents and the school knew he was faking, but "just didn't know what to do about it." By sixth grade, he estimates that he was missing "at least thirty days per year of school — maybe more."

By sixth and seventh grades, John remembers that "the anxiety really hit hard — there were classes full of new people, and I couldn't handle it." He frequently ended up in the guidance counselor's office in tears, and his mother would come to take him home. Later in high school, the guidance personnel tried to place him in a special needs room at school, but he was embarrassed by this and refused to go. John dropped out of high school at age sixteen. He is now twenty-four, and has no job, no social life, and no plans. He passed the test for his learner's permit, but never took the road test and never got his driver's license. The only time he leaves his home is for a doctor's appointment. "I have no life," he says.

Certainly, John's is a story of extreme social anxiety and how debilitating it can be. But there's another layer to the story for us to look at as well. John has played video games ever since he can remember. It started with simple one-player games at age five or six. He would either play when he came home from school, or, occasionally, go to a neighbor's house and game. On the days he faked being sick, he remembers that he would "just come home from school and turn it on." By the time he was ten, the games had become more sophisticated, the gaming time had extended, and although his parents made rules, they "didn't enforce them."

When John reached seventh grade, the games went online. "It was addictive before," he says, "but online brings it to a whole new level." It was also about this time that he stopped eating dinner with his parents and started bringing food to his room. With the arrival of online gaming, the amount of screen time exploded to "at least four hours per day on weekdays, and much more on weekends." Going to bed became a hotly contested issue in the family. By the time John arrived at my office, he had been out of school for years. He was gaming as many as sixteen hours per day, frequently staying up until two or three in the morning. John has no social contacts of any kind outside of gaming, and none of the people with whom he games does he see in person. Lately, he has started to spend hours watching YouTube videos of other people playing the games that he plays. He picked this up when his parents — as they have periodically attempted to do — set some limits on gaming, but not on internet use. John's parents, both extremely concerned for his welfare, have nevertheless been unable to establish and follow through on a course of action. They know that the gaming is unhealthy, but feel that "it's all he has," and that "he'd be so depressed without it." As I write this, John himself has decided that he "isn't ready yet" to work on his anxiety, and he has dropped out of treatment.

As you can see, John's version of anxiety is extraordinarily passive. If you met him, you would just think he was quiet and reserved. And passively and quietly, he has slipped beneath the surface of life, leaving hardly a ripple. But sometimes, even though the central dynamic is still anxiety, the whole process looks completely different. Let me introduce you now to Sam, and we'll see what this looks like in a more aggressive presentation.

Sam

Sam came to me at the age of thirteen, a seventh grader with a diagnosis of attention deficit hyperactivity disorder. His parents described him as disorganized and defiant. "He never does his homework — we can't trust him — he lies about

100

everything — we tell him to do things, and he just says no."
According to Sam, "They have a lot of rules. It doesn't mean
I follow them." Sam's parents had very fundamental disagreements about what the rules should be and acknowledged that
they overcompensated for each other. Sam himself made no
secret of the fact that he manipulated his parents to get what
he wanted. He came to his appointments in a hooded sweat-
shirt, and he was manifestly angry and anxious. But, unexpect-
edly, he quickly adjusted to coming to therapy and, when we
were alone, he said, "I want to succeed, but only on *my* terms.
I don't want help, and I don't want to be told what to do."

Academically, Sam struggled through middle and high school.
He always seemed to be on the edge of collapse, but he never
gave up and always did just enough work to get by. And he
never skipped school. "If I ever said to my parents that I didn't
feel good, they'd say 'suck it up and go to school.'" Socially, he
was withdrawn. He never dated and never participated in a
single extracurricular activity. He was, however, on the fringe
of a particular group at school, all of whom had one thing in
common: gaming.

Sam's gaming started early: "as soon as I was sentient," in
his memorable wording. He had a PlayStation and hand-
held games in the early years, and, up through third grade,
he played with friends. However, in fourth grade, his family
moved to a town where he had no friends, and "that's when it
really set in." After school, he would simply come home and
game. His parents were concerned, and they "tried to make
rules, but didn't follow through. They'd say, 'If you don't do

your homework, we'll take the game away," but even when they did, they only took one device. There were always others. It was only words."

Sam first gamed online with Xbox in seventh grade, and it was a revelation for him, as he discovered that "there's a zillion people like me." He recalls getting home from school at 2:30, grabbing a snack, gaming until early morning, and then going to bed to catch a few hours of sleep before school. His family never ate together; when he was hungry, he would get something to eat and take it to his room. Interestingly, however, Sam did not evolve (or perhaps devolve) to a position of solely gaming with people he never met. On the contrary, as he went through high school, "it became more important to game with people who were actually around me." Also, he was unusually attached to the process of psychotherapy, insisting on keeping regular appointments even over vacation times.

As I write this, Sam is twenty-one. He graduated from high school on time, with not much academic margin for error, to put it mildly. He lives at home, but works approximately forty hours per week at a job with very few intellectual demands, but which calls for consistent contact with the public. He has his driver's license, and in fact loves the independence of driving. His plan is to get a job driving trucks or vans, which he feels would give him a shot at a career, as opposed to his current "dead end" job, but would also be tolerable from the standpoint of his anxiety. He has one close friend and a few acquaintances. Until recently, he had a "girlfriend," who lived 3,000 miles from his home and with whom his contact was exclusively electronic. Recently, however, he has come to terms with the reality that there is no real substance (let alone a future) to that relationship. At our last session, he had downloaded, for the first time, a dating app on his phone. He hasn't contacted anyone yet. We'll see. I guess the thought counts for something. But in the meantime, he games every moment he is not working or sleeping.

As you can see, Sam's struggles through his teen years were similar in some ways to John's, but manifested differently. Notice also that although he pulled back from his family, he was always connected to some degree with at least a couple of people in the outside world. Also, since he never left school, he was constantly forced to deal with and adapt to social situations that made him anxious. He is certainly debilitated, but considerably less so than John.

Now let's have a look at Taylor, whose anxiety came out in symptoms, and for whom gaming played a somewhat less central role.

Taylor

Taylor came to my office for the first time at the age of sixteen, at the suggestion of his pediatrician. He had a history of headaches dating back to fourth grade, and had been diagnosed with migraine and tension headaches and allergies. His symptoms (in addition to headaches) included sensitivity to light, vomiting, dizziness, and double vision. His medication history included trials of Wellbutrin, Elavil, Tylenol #3, Diamox, Prilosec, Topamax, and Imitrex. He had seen, in addition to

103

his primary physician and a neurologist at a major teaching hospital, a massage therapist, a hypnotherapist, and an acupuncturist. Taylor had missed significant time at school over the years, but most of the absences had been excused for medical reasons. Because he was an excellent student, he had not fallen behind academically. Taylor showed up for treatment in a wheelchair (for his dizziness) wearing dark, wraparound sunglasses (for his light sensitivity).

In the later years of high school, Taylor showed slow and steady symptomatic improvement. He abandoned the wheelchair and glasses, and his attendance at school improved. His social life was extremely limited, but he did stay connected to music, playing in the jazz ensembles at his school. He graduated on time, and enrolled at a college located about two hours from his home.

Initially, Taylor did well at college, and his physical symptoms remained under control. However, during his sophomore year, he started to have academic problems. He developed a pattern of putting off long-term assignments, skipping classes (because the work wasn't done), falling further behind, panicking, and withdrawing further. When his parents, who kept in good touch with him, asked how he was doing, he lied and led them to believe all was going well. From time to time, he would go "radio silent," allowing his phone to run out of battery, so that he wouldn't be asked questions he didn't want to answer. Because he was over eighteen years old, his parents did not have automatic access to his grades, and they felt that asking for that access would convey a lack of trust.

Over time, as I'm sure you have guessed, the house of cards came tumbling down. As his parents prepared for the semester in which they thought he would graduate, Taylor finally had to admit that he was approximately two years behind in credits. He dropped out of school and returned home, mortified and discouraged. However, in spite of their disappointment, his parents continued to be patient and supportive. Recognizing that he was not ready to simply try again at school, Taylor took a full-time minimum wage job in an office supply store and settled into the business of simply meeting the requirements of a steady and consistent job. After a year, he began classes at a local college, while continuing to live at home. Now, a year later, he is starting back as a full-time student, and is optimistic that he will be able to graduate in a year, at age twenty-seven. So far this semester, he has attended all his classes and passed in the homework. I think he'll do it.

On the topic of the internet and gaming, Taylor has an interesting perspective. He agrees that social anxiety always lay at the core of his problems, but notes that "I didn't only lose myself in internet games. I spent hours on Xbox and Nintendo, but also I slept and read." He remembers having friends who disappeared into World of Warcraft, but he (as odd as this may seem) found that sort of game *too* social, and preferred the total isolation of books and individual games. "Reading," he says, "was as obsessive for me as gaming was for some of my friends." Interestingly, from his current perspective, Taylor feels that the modifications made by his high school to deal with his symptoms, well intentioned though they were, were in fact harmful, because they made it "easier

105

to stay home. If I had been forced to go to school, I wouldn't have responded well, but I would have learned to live with it. My parents let me stay home. They made it easy for me to retreat from social situations. It was meant for the best, but it was counterproductive."

As you can see, gaming, for Taylor, formed a part of his retreat from the normal flow of life, but did not consume him, in the way it has Sam and John. He did not, in short, become an addict. And he is much closer to recovery than the other two young men.

• • •

What do we take from all of this? As always, there are no simple conclusions to be drawn. And, to be honest, there are certainly many worse situations than those I describe here, because my sample comes from families who are involved enough to bring their child to a psychologist. But we can probably draw some conclusions. We can say that at one end of the spectrum, gaming can be an enjoyable break from the routine of school, sports, and other organized activities. At the other, it can be addictive and destructive. (And there is probably a place in the middle, where it could go either way.) We can say that gaming is largely flying under the parenting radar, probably because the kids are safe, quiet, and not hung over in the morning. But I think we should also say this: particularly in combination with anxiety, gaming can distort and radically alter the life of a child. And like all addictions, it can weave itself into the fabric of both an individual life and the life of a family. With devastating results.

What do you do about it? Just what we said earlier. Set limits, both on the days allowed for gaming and on the length of gaming sessions. No gaming within an hour of bedtime. No gaming options (of any sort) taken to the bedroom at night. No gaming if your child is staying home from school. If he's too sick to study, he's too sick to game. Running away from social anxiety into a world of virtual friendships will not work; don't fall for the illusion that it is working. Watch carefully as your child enters this world. There are very real dangers here, and they won't necessarily be obvious as they emerge. Nobody wants to end up being John. You may trust me when I tell you that John himself doesn't want to be John.

Driving, Drinking, Drugs, Sex, and More Food

Well, these are certainly interesting topics. Maybe your child won't have a problem with any of them. Maybe. But just in case, let's have a look.

Driving

Start with driving. Although you may dread its approach, ultimately you will arrive at the day when decisions need to be made about driving. Your best plan is to anticipate this day well in advance, and discuss its ramifications with your child. For obvious reasons, this is one of the most important issues you will face in the teen years. It is the first time that you place in your child's hands the ability, with just a moment's carelessness, to kill or cripple himself or someone else. All your conversations and rules should reflect this.

The internet has lent an immediacy to our sense of expectation for the pace at which things happen: Order it! Get it delivered! Put it on the card! All of which is fine, when the topic is resupplying the house with laundry detergent. None of which is fine when we're talking about driving. I confess to watching in horror as some parents pay for their child's driver's education, buy him a car, pay for his insurance, hand him the keys, and turn him loose. This casual approach to such a critical issue is a mistake with potentially fatal consequences. If your child is eager to drive, start discussing the topic at least a year in advance. Decide what his financial contribution will be, and ensure that accruing the money takes time, effort, and self-control (i.e., delay of gratification). Does he buy the car? Does he pay for driver's ed or for insurance? Whatever you decide, it should take work, saving, and planning. A child who has held a job, delayed his own immediate gratification to set aside money, carefully planned his priorities, and acted on that plan will, quite simply, make a safer driver. "Birthday money" and "allowance money" and other unearned income sources do not teach the same lessons. Saving for a car is yet another way of teaching the critical fact that actions have consequences. Spend the money you earn, and it takes longer to get on the road. (And by the way, why would a person old enough to drive be getting an allowance? An allowance is a gift from a generous parent to a child who is not old enough to get a job. If you're old enough to drive, you're old enough to get a job.) As a parent, your own financial resources are not the question here. Regardless of how much money you have, do not gift your child the ability to drive. Make him earn it. If it slows down the process, so be it.

Before your child goes on the road, you'll need to think about the basic rules. At the outset, you are finding out if your child can handle this task at a very basic level. And without intending to be overly dramatic, you must remember that the downside risk of being wrong about your child's readiness is her death. Is she casual about safety? Does she drive too fast or too close to the car in front of her? If you find that she's not ready for this responsibility, that's fine. Wait a while, and try again. Do not hesitate to take back your child's license or permit if she shows signs of irresponsibility. The state may say she can drive. That doesn't mean you are required to let her.

What are signs of irresponsibility? Certainly, the examples mentioned above would qualify. Others include taking friends in the car when he shouldn't, any signs of emotionality (especially anger) reflected in driving behavior, and any indication whatsoever of drugs or alcohol having been in the car. These are obvious, and should be met with immediate restrictions. Take his license. Never mind that he needs his car to get to school or to his job. You figured it out before he had his license. Figure it out again.

Let's look in particular at smart phone use in the car. No one is going to like my position on this one, but here it is: for at least the first month of solo driving, turn the phone off. Never mind Bluetooth. Never mind Apple Car Play. Turn it off. Driving safely is a complex skill, and experienced drivers are doing a lot of things to keep themselves safe, most of which have become automatic. But it takes time to make them automatic, and the phone is a potentially fatal distraction. Turn it off. If your child forgot to tell you something, or you forgot to tell her something, do what people have always done: wait. Even

111

the radio or a playlist may be too much of a distraction for a beginner. The phone certainly is.

Driving with a GPS is a specific skill that needs practice as well. Certainly, it is a valuable aid to navigation, and a lot better than trying to read a map while driving (remember that?). However, you have to take your eyes off the road to use it, and that's dangerous for a new driver. When you are doing your practice driving hours with your child, go to an unknown destination that requires a series of turns. Have her make a wrong turn on purpose, and allow the GPS to help her recover. This may seem overcautious to your child. It's not.

Additionally, today's technology allows you to track your new teen driver. You can monitor location, speed, time of use, and all the other relevant parameters. When you do it, as you certainly should, your child will say that you do not trust him, etc., etc. Same old stuff. Tell him this isn't a moral issue, it's a safety issue. Tell him that you model yourself after Ronald Reagan: "trust but verify." Tell him that if he's a careful driver who only goes where he says he's going, what difference does it make? Tell him whatever you want, but use the technology until you're convinced you no longer need it.

At a less critical level, you will also need to establish day-to-day norms and curfews. Once again, be clear, consistent, and set the rules and punishers in advance. If you have said, "Be home by 10 p.m." on a Friday night, and she comes home at 10:10, she is late. Apply the punisher (perhaps loss of the vehicle for a weekend night). Why be so strict? If you let ten minutes go, how about fifteen? Twenty? When does it stop? You establish that 10 p.m. means 10 p.m. If she runs into an unavoidable problem, she can call and get permission to come home later. If she does not call, then she is expected home. You are doing two things here. On the one hand, you are handling the practical problem of getting your child home at the time you feel is appropriate. On the other, you are conveying the message that permission to drive is serious business and will be handled seriously. All safety-related rules should be handled with the same degree of seriousness.

Drugs

Now to drugs. From the perspective of parenting decisions, since drug and alcohol issues arrive at the same time as driving, it makes sense to look at them together. What should the specific rules be? Let's start with the obvious: no drug use of any kind while driving. No drug use of any kind by anyone else who is in the car. No transportation of drugs or alcohol by you or anyone in the car with you. Any transgressions of these rules will result in your taking away your child's license. No second chances, and no excuses. Any evidence whatsoever of transgressions means your child is not yet ready. Six months is a reasonable penalty. Do it.

But what about grey areas? Can he, for example, drive to parties or events where *other* people are using substances? There's a wide variety of thinking on this topic. Some parents try to insulate their children from making any of these decisions, and simply say no. Others don't even address the issue,

113

or else make vague references to "good decision making," without clearly stating what those decisions should be. This is not the time to be vague. This is the time to have clear and specific discussions.

And if we're going to discuss this clearly, we need to ask ourselves what our goal is. There is nothing we, as parents, can do about the prevalence of alcohol, marijuana, and other drugs in our culture. Some communities do a better job than others of limiting the availability, but the reality is that any teenager who goes to parties or other evening events will, at some point, have decisions to make. Our goal, then, is for our children to be able to intelligently handle themselves in situations where their peers are not. The complication is that even smart people make stupid decisions when it comes to drugs, sex, and alcohol, or any combination thereof. Especially (although not exclusively) during the teenage years. This is why we set limits during the teenage years, hoping our kids grow brains before we turn them loose. However, once again, you want these limits to be set in a dispassionate and respectful manner, transmitting as clearly as possible that they are not arbitrary and capricious, but are designed to respond to real and substantial risks. You are again trying to maximize the chance of these limits being internalized and becoming a part of your child's own value system.

Returning to the grey areas we noted above, we must recognize that much depends on where you are in your journey through adolescence with your teen. If she lies about homework or cleaning her room or other relatively minor things — if you don't trust her in general — then why in the world would you trust her on the critically important issues of substances and driving? As you will explain to her on dozens of occasions, trust is a commodity that takes months and years to build but that can be lost in an instant. If you are in the relatively early stages of trust (which is to say that you, in your heart, don't believe that your child is capable of making consistently safe choices when confronted with dangerous options), then make rules. Set relatively early curfews. Check to see if adults are home at the places your child is going. Track her phone and car. Do your best to keep her away from choices she is not yet ready to make. She will be angry with you. Again. You will say: "If you want freedom, you must build trust." She will say: "How long does that take?" You will say: "One day at a time." She will say: "How am I supposed to build trust if you won't let me do anything?" You will say: "There are a million ways to build trust. Do your homework and chores without being asked. Be where you say you will be, and be on time. Pick up your stuff. Treat the people around you with respect." You will think of other examples. These are difficult conversations, and they often don't go well, but if you can stay away from anger, they are important components of the transition to adulthood, as well as the elements of the plan to keep your child safe.

When you do get to a point of greater trust, then your situation has changed, and it's time to ask yourself this question: if your child is capable of driving to a party (or simply being at a party) where other people are abusing substances, but not do so himself, then why is it not ok for him to go? After all, we are not trying to raise other people's children. And since

115

we have limited ability to change the culture, these situations will present themselves. If your child tells you he wants to go to a party where there will likely be drinking, but gives you his word that he will not drink — and if you trust him — then why would you say no? In fact, wouldn't your child's ability to control himself in the face of temptation be a better outcome than lockdown restriction? If signs that he broke his word emerge, then you reset the trust dial. Lock down. Say no. And start the slow process of rebuilding trust.

In the big picture, the effort here is to remove at least some of the arbitrariness of the rule establishment process, and to make it responsive to the evolution of the teen's ability to control her behavior. However, let's be clear that this is categorically not the same thing as blindly trusting and hoping for the best. This approach only makes sense if you take immediate and decisive action at the first sign that trust has been broken. Remember what is at stake here: your child's life. No "second chances." No "we'll let it slide this once." No "we'll keep this between us and not tell your mother." No "everyone makes mistakes." Drinking and driving is not a "mistake." Neither component happened accidentally. If your child cannot yet handle a situation, then it is your job to keep her out of that situation until she's ready.

I frequently speak with parents who have, in one form or another, given up on the concept of limit setting during adolescence. They say: "All kids experiment during the teen years." Or, "They're going to do it anyway, so they might as well do it in a safe place." In fact, I have often heard parents speak with pride of taking car keys from teens who are partying at their house, as though this represented a piece of responsible parenting. Do we not see that kids will get the message that it is not only ok that they drink, but that it's expected? Ironically, parents of athletes seem often to be particularly susceptible to the fantasy that their children, perhaps by virtue of their athleticism, are exempt from the danger of addiction. This brand of thinking is misguided and dangerous. Addiction is not a disease of the stupid, of the poor, or of the uncoordinated. Exposure to addictive drugs at an early age raises the risk of addiction. Alcohol is one of the addictive drugs in question. The fact that it is legal at twenty-one is, in this context, irrelevant. There are tens of millions of alcohol addicts who could attest to this. We should not be implying to our children, either overtly or covertly, that it is either ok with us or inevitable that they drink or smoke as teenagers. On the contrary, we should do everything we can to encourage them to put off experimenting for as long as possible, giving their brains the maximum time to develop in the absence of psychoactive drugs, and improving as much as possible the odds that they will make those legendary "good decisions."

As an aside, I don't waste my time in meaningless discussion about whether marijuana is "as addictive as" or "addictive in the same way as" alcohol (discussions frequently fueled by some dubious "research" gleaned from some equally dubious website). The fact is that there are many people for whom marijuana, in whatever form, has become an integral part of their lives, who would have a great deal of difficulty stopping its use, and on whose lives it has had major impact. If we're

117

not calling that "addiction" in some technical sense, fine. For the purpose of the discussions I have with teens, it's close enough. As I write this, marijuana is legal for recreational and medical use in some jurisdictions, and I do not doubt that this trend will continue. And I also do not doubt that when all the evidence is in, we will find that the earlier you start using, the more likely it is that its use will be a problem in your life. As a parent, I suggest you treat it the same as you do alcohol: don't permit its use by your teens, and don't imply that this fits into some covert "don't ask don't tell" semi-permission limbo. Same, by the way, with nicotine in all its forms. Including Juuling, which as I write this is becoming ridiculously popular, and is going to give us a whole new crop of nicotine addicts. If you don't know what Juuling (or vaping in general) is, then look it up. Or ask your child.

Please note that in neither the case of alcohol nor that of marijuana do I make a moral case to teens. I am not suggesting that their friends who smoke and drink are necessarily "bad" (although they may be bad influences). On the contrary, I understand their desire to experiment, and their confidence that they personally will be able to keep drug use under control. But I also understand that not a single one of the twelve million or so alcoholics in the U.S. thought that he would become an alcoholic when he started experimenting with alcohol. So the confidence of a sixteen-year-old that he can "handle it" is not persuasive to me. I think he is more likely to make sound decisions when he is twenty-one. So I make rules — once again, not out of anger or rigidity or a desire to be in control, but because I am contracted to be the best parent I can be. If it's of any use to you, here's what I actually say to teens about drinking: "Alcohol is an addictive drug. Anyone who drinks is participating in an experiment, entitled 'can I use an addictive drug for fun, but not become an addict.' Some people can, and some can't, and there's no way to know in advance to which group you belong. There are certain circumstances that increase the chances you'll become an addict: 1) if you have an addict in your family; 2) if you start early; 3) if you do it a lot. I can't do much about your genetics, but I'll fight you all the way through high school to decrease your other risk factors. Because I do not want you coming to me as a twenty-five-year-old with a substance problem and asking me why I didn't have the guts to take a stand when you were fifteen." Of course, there's no way to know if this approach works better than other efforts at deterrence. But the teens I work with seem at least willing to listen. Without rolling their eyes.

Regarding alcohol, marijuana, and nicotine, I'm sorry to tell you that scare tactics and dire warnings about health consequences will generally have no effect. Teens are not afraid of those drugs. They have too much exposure. They are too widely used — often in the child's own home. I'm not saying I am opposed to providing information. Go ahead and give them the facts. But I am not convinced, given the ubiquity of these drugs in our society, that this approach will result in behavior change. (*We* knew we shouldn't do it when we were teens. We did it anyway, when we could get away with it.) Instead, you can make the logical and well-grounded case described above. You want to be measured, consistent,

119

dispassionate, and relentless. You may be assured that in most parts of the country, teen culture is not helping you out. Regrettably, in many cases, your adult neighbors are not helping you out either. There has been, over the years, a steady erosion in parents' willingness to take a stand in these areas, and I am not going to explore the roots of this phenomenon. I am simply saying that it's a mistake. Brain development hasn't changed, and kids don't make any better decisions than they ever did.

Drugs other than alcohol, marijuana, and nicotine require a different approach. The benzodiazepines (e.g., Xanax), ecstasy, cocaine, the opiates, the hallucinogens, etc. can be attacked with more passion and less risk that your child will tune you out. Nobody romanticizes opioid use. It is inevitable, if regrettable, that in most communities, our children will eventually be at parties where their friends are drinking or smoking. It is equally inevitable that, at the age of twenty-one, they will need to decide whether alcohol and nicotine (and likely marijuana) will play a legal recreational part in their lives. It is not at all inevitable that this will be the case with snorting coke or dropping acid or taking Oxycodone. Tell your child that if she finds herself in situations where such things are happening, she needs to leave. Immediately. Tell her that she is not allowed to associate with kids who are doing those things. And when you end up in the "you can't choose my friends" discussion, say, "On this issue, I can and I will." And then do everything you can to enforce your position. You would rather have your child not speak to you for a decade out of anger and resent than to have her be an opiate addict.

Sex

What about sex? Well, *there's* a question. Let's back up a bit and get some perspective. In a practical book like this, we're not going to spend much time on the morality of premarital sex, the relationship of sex to love, the synergy between physical and emotional closeness, and other related philosophical topics. It's not that these aren't important, and it's certainly not that these aren't valuable discussions to have with our teenagers. On the contrary, they should be going on all the time, and be grounded in your values, and your religious and spiritual beliefs. We'll touch on these briefly below, but as always, it's not my business here to tell you what your beliefs should be. We have taken on a far more prosaic task: to figure out, in the general case, how to approach the topic with kids, and what the rules should be.

We need to start with a couple of basic observations. First, even smart and well-grounded people do stupid things when it comes to sex. They know better. They feel guilty afterward. They wish they hadn't done it. But they do it. Your child is unlikely to be immune. Second, if I may state the obvious, males and females are infrequently on the same page with respect to the sexual aspects of relationships. This would be less of a problem if each side didn't fantasize that the other thinks about sex the same way that they do. But that will never happen. I have no intention here of either condemning or excusing any behavior. Rather, I am observing the obvious fact that sexual attraction is a real and powerful force. If we leave teenage people who are sexually attracted to each other

121

unsupervised, alone, and in the dark, there will probably be sexual activity. If alcohol or other drugs are also present, this becomes even more likely. (You will note that my phrasing is gender neutral. The same applies to gay teens and bi teens and any other gender identity you might care to name.) If we don't want this to happen, we must supervise. If the gathering is at someone else's house, we need to make sure an adult is present — and not one of those adults who goes to bed at nine when the party lasts until eleven.

Let's state one thing clearly: teenage girls in unsupervised situations with teenage boys are at risk for being forced (or coerced, which is a close relative of forced) to do things that they don't want to do, or are ambivalent about doing. I understand that I am at risk for sounding sexist or paternalistic at this juncture, but that is not the intent. It is a simple function of size and strength that boys can force girls more easily than girls can force boys. No societal progress we may make in the teaching of respect and ethics to young men (which we most certainly should attempt), or in the strengthening of self-esteem and self-respect in young women, will alter that fact. Keep your daughter out of these situations. I understand that in families with both sons and daughters, this opens us up to the critique of having a "double standard"; but my contention is that this is an issue of common sense. A 5'9" 170-pound boy dating a 5'2" 100-pound girl is not uncommon, and is the physical equivalent in relative size of that same boy dating a 6'4" 240-pound girl. Which *is* uncommon. Were that to happen, I might be equally cautious about the boy.

Parenthetically, there are indeed situations in which we need to bring extra caution to the table for our boys as well. For example, men are more likely than women to use recreational drugs of all sorts, and are more likely to end up in emergency rooms and die as a result. They are also worse drivers: they get more tickets for reckless driving, drive drunk more often, and die at double the rate of women in car crashes. Common sense, therefore, dictates stricter and more cautious rules for boys in these areas.

But it is also in this context incredibly important that you and your spouse treat each other with the kind of respect that serves as a template for your child's relationships in general, and his intimate relationships in particular. After all, respectful sexual behavior is a subset of respectful behavior in general. If all disrespectful behavior is off the table in all situations, then it follows that it's off the table in sexual situations as well. Many cultural traditions seem to have done a miserable job at getting this across to their boys. "Locker room talk" is the precursor to locker room think, which in turn is the precursor to abusive behavior. It's unacceptable. Even in a locker room. Teach your children that they are responsible for their behavior. Period.

What does all this mean about the rules you should have regarding sex? Look, there are a million discussions to have, about morals and ethics and STDs and pregnancy and self-respect and intimacy and communication and on and on. And you should have them all, many times over. But no matter what you say, in the battle between the intellect and the sex

123

drive, the winner — brace yourself — will not always be the intellect. They'll think they're "ready" before you think they are. They'll think it's "love," when you think it's infatuation. And most of the time, as has always been true, there won't be much in the way of "thinking" going on at all. What is left for us to do? Well, that depends on what your goal is. As we have said elsewhere, unsupervised teenagers, left alone, do things they wouldn't do if adults were watching. Do we know where full-on sexual activity takes place? Sure we do. Sleepovers. Parties. Bonfires. After school and before you get home. At the beach. In the woods. In cars. And, of course, on prom night. Technology hasn't changed any of this. These are the same places you snuck out to. If you don't want your teenager to have sex with his girlfriend, don't let him be unsupervised in those sorts of situations.

Do I think you can realistically stop all sexual contact for your teen? Of course not. I'd bet teens were successfully sneaking out of their caves 10,000 years ago. But do I think you should just bow to the inevitable? No, I do not. Why not? Well, lots of reasons. First, there's no infallible method of contraception, and your teen is not ready to be a parent. And you, presumably, don't want another baby. Second, STDs. We live in the age of AIDS and HPV (not to mention all the old favorites from when you were growing up). If you don't know much about these viral diseases, get busy and find out. Both are present in the sexually active teenage population. Both can have life-long implications. Both are, in short, very bad news. (And by the way, if you are saying to yourself that condoms can mitigate the risk of some of this stuff, good for you. You're right.

They can. But only when they are used and used properly. The bad news is that kids are as dumb as ever when it comes to sexual behavior. Those of us who were doing sex education back in the eighties thought that AIDS would change that, and that kids would smarten up. No such luck. They still have unprotected sex, and lots of it.) And if the health and pregnancy concerns aren't enough to convince you to take a stand, consider the whole host of relationship issues, which might be summed up as follows: sex between teens virtually never makes a relationship better. Boys and girls aren't on the same page. Someone gets hurt. Usually the girl.

Does this mean it's a waste of time to educate your teen about condoms and STDs and the rest of it? Of course not. This is critical information for a teen to have. Anyone who thinks that supplying a teen with knowledge about sex implies condoning indiscriminate (or even discriminate) sex hasn't spent near enough time talking to his kids. But information isn't enough. If you don't think your teen should have sex, say so, and say why not. Make it clear that, although you are aware that you can't be in complete control and you understand that she might disagree with you, she does not have your permission, let alone your blessing. Say "no" to her putting herself in situations like those described above.

We'll get back to the rules in a minute, but here's the brief philosophical interlude I promised above: learning how to integrate a physical relationship with an emotional relationship is one of the great lessons of life, and it must be learned at some point. The truth is, many adults who blame their repeated relationship failures on not having found the "right person" have misunderstood the problem. Without the right skill set, there is no right person. With the right skill set, there are lots of right people. Integrating physical and emotional intimacy is part of that skill set. But when are you supposed to start learning it, if not during the teen years? Here, then, is the paradox: we don't want our teenage children having sex. But not only is it absurd to think that we could control every dark corner and back seat, it's not clear that we would want to even if we could, because they have to figure this stuff out. Not that long ago, we handled this by essentially saying: "You're not allowed to do anything until you're married. Figure it out then. In the meantime, keep your hands to yourself." It didn't work, of course, but I do not doubt that this approach saved those folks from a lot of difficult parenting. And I'm well aware that there are many people who still think that's the right path. I think it's simplistic.

At the same time, today's brand of "look the other way" parenting doesn't do our kids any good either. There *are* moral issues here. There are questions of right and wrong, self-respect, respect for others, power and exploitation, and a million other areas where kids need our help and guidance. It's complex and difficult, but why would that surprise us? And why are we willing to have countless brutal conversations about grades and homework, but try to do this subject in one "talk"? This is just another part of the parenting job. No matter how awkward the conversations are, have them.

Returning, then, to the "rules" question, the answer is as complex as the topic. It depends, as it usually does, on where you are with your child at the moment in question. When he's fourteen, you'll be restrictive. When he's eighteen, less so. If she's immature and impulsive, you'll be more restrictive. If she's insightful, responsible in other areas, and able to talk reasonably about this stuff, you'll back off to some degree. You will make every effort to keep your child out of decision-making situations for which he is not prepared, and you will be savvy enough to know what those situations are. I wish I could give you a list of rules and a matched list of ages at which to apply them. No such luck.

Food

Last but far from least, I'm going to return to questions of food and eating. However, I'm not going to pretend for an instant that this is going to be a comprehensive treatment of the topic. Why not? It's just too complex. If you really want to get an overview, you'd need to explore questions of culture, media, sexuality, peer influences, family dynamics, control, anger, and a host of other issues. The study of body image alone has generated a vast literature, including exploration of sexual abuse, athleticism, the importance of attractiveness, body dysmorphic conditions, obesity, anorexia, and dozens of other perspectives. As I noted earlier, this is one area where, if you are having some serious concerns about your child, you should consider getting professional help from someone with experience in the area. But how are you to tell if your concerns are "serious"? Let's have a look at that.

127

The symptoms of eating problems are what you would expect: binge eating, undereating, purging, and obsession with food, body image, or weight. But it's not always that obvious. Sometimes there's compulsive exercise. Sometimes there's weight loss, but you have no idea why. Almost always there's a connection with anxiety, but sometimes that's well hidden — concealed behind a reluctance (or refusal) to even talk about the issue. Now, if you are an experienced observer of teens, you will be saying to yourself that most of these symptoms are relatively common, and many times they resolve on their own — and that's true enough. It's a question of degree. Attempting to eat a healthy diet is fine. Self-starvation is not. Working out is fine. Multi-hour, daily aerobic workouts are not. Weighing oneself once a week and keeping track of it is fine. Weighing oneself four times a day is not. Being disappointed about breaking a diet is fine. Shame, guilt, and fear of loss of control is not. Purging is never fine. It comes down, as it so often does, to the degree of disturbance of relationships (both within and outside the family) and of altered achievement at school. A symptom of serious degree should trigger action. A noticeable disruption of function should do the same. You should know that some of the dysfunctional behaviors associated with eating problems (e.g., purging) can become powerful habits that are extremely difficult to break once established, and can cause serious health issues. You would rather take action that turns out to have been unnecessary than to have mild eating issues turn into major ones.

Our normal arsenal of behavioral technology, I'm sorry to say, does not work with serious eating issues. That's because of the tricky emotional factors that are involved. If you have a teen-age girl for whom you think this might be an issue, read some of the "pro-anorexia" blogs on the web, to get a feel for the emotional landscape. Here, for example, is the briefest hint at the complexity of the problem: if we make "rules" about eating for a child who feels fat, disgusting, and out of control whenever she eats, then we are, from *her* perspective, pun-ishing her. We are "forcing" her to eat, which robs her of the sense of control that she so desperately seeks. If in turn she is angry at you for forcing her to eat, she can "punish" you by not eating. In other words, as long as it is a battle of wills, we will make no progress. Instead, we must locate, nurture, and engage the healthiest and strongest part of the child, so that she can work *with* us. That's not easy to do, which is the reason to seek the help of professionals. (Recently, a fourteen-year-old with whom I was working on eating problems, when she learned that her pediatrician was considering hospitaliz-ing her, texted to a friend: "Let them *try* to make me eat!". To her, help will feel like an assault. This will be difficult.)

Summary

The teen years comprise an extraordinarily difficult and chal-lenging time of life, with dozens of complex factors involved in high-stakes decision making. I've tried to make some sug-gestions, based on general principles and normative teen behavior. But in the final analysis, you know your own chil-dren, and you are the best judge of how to tailor the rules for your individual situation. Your children will push you away during these years, because that is what they need to do to become autonomous adults. Don't get angry in response. Quietly, consistently, and relentlessly, stick to your guns. As we have already noted, your job is not to be their buddy when they're fifteen. It is to be able to look them in the eye when they are twenty-five and say that you were always the best parent you could figure out how to be. Even when they said they hated you. Conflict is an almost inevitable by-product of doing a good job of parenting. The fact that there is conflict is often painful, but doesn't mean that you're doing it wrong, and may well mean the opposite. The project, once again, is to engender and support in our children the evolution of sound values and the ability to make decisions based on those values, while protecting them from disaster while that evolution is in progress. It's not easy.

College, Letting Go, and Boomerangs

Well, here we are, finally. We've done our best to do the "roots" part of the job, and now it's time for "wings." By comparison, this should be the easier of the two, right? Sorry. It doesn't work that way. And the digital age has, if anything, made it harder. Let's have a look.

The first challenge is that this part is counterintuitive. Not unlike when we send our children off to the tender mercies of the educational system at age five or six, it doesn't feel right. We know they'll make mistakes. We remember the mistakes *we* made, and that we are lucky to still be alive. We don't want them to make the same ones. We want to protect them. Well, it didn't work with us, and it won't work with them. At some (indeterminate) age, our kids just need to learn things for themselves. They need to feel the pain and recover. Sometimes, they need to make the mistake and pay the price. And sometimes, through no fault of their own, tough things happen, and they need to figure out what to do about it.

As parents, the hard thing to remember is that this is what we *want* to happen. We do not want our children to be dependent on us. We would like them to *want* to be in touch with us, but not to *need* to be in touch with us. When a young adult solves a problem by herself, she not only owns the solution to that problem, she owns the knowledge that she can solve the next problem. And that knowledge is priceless. You don't get it from a lecture.

However, none of this — as clearly rational as it may be — relieves the fear of a conscientious parent watching her child emerge from the relative safety of the home into a callous and dangerous world. The number of horrifying outcomes, in the mind of a parent with even a moderate imagination, is limitless. Nevertheless, let's remember that this is exactly the point of all that conscientious parenting. This was the hidden agenda behind all those rules, all that calm consistency, and all those efforts to strike a balance between freedom and responsibility during the teen years. As we have said on many occasions, it has never solely been about homework or a clean room or a reasonable bedtime. It has been about the internalization of a value system that our children will ultimately use to make decisions in their own lives. Let's be clear here: we do our children no favors by continuing to make decisions for them past the age when they can make them for themselves. And we do them no favors by protecting them from the consequences of the bad decisions that they do make. On the contrary, that's the definition of enabling, and it quite literally slows down the maturation process. I recently was involved in a situation in which a young man made some poor driving decisions, which resulted in totaling his car. His parents bought him a new one, reasoning that he needed it to get to school. I understand that his having a car was more convenient for them. But what, do we suppose, was the lesson learned here by the child?

There's another aspect of this wings project that needs mentioning: the impact of a child leaving home on a parent who, for the last eighteen years, has had "parent" as the primary (or sole) job description. It's a complicated question. We all define ourselves in part by what we do with our time. When we change (or stop) what we are doing, it has an impact on our internal lives. (This is the reason that many people have a much harder time with retirement than they anticipated. They don't know who they are anymore, or what to do with their time.) Parenting is no different. While our children are home, being a parent is why we get up in the morning. It is, as we have said, challenging, time-consuming, and poorly compensated — but it's a huge job. And yet, after eighteen years of outstanding and thankless service, you get fired. Just like that. The kid leaves home. What now?

Let's not pretend we can solve this problem. It's not "solvable" in any meaningful sense. The only way a parent can escape a sense of loss (both personal and existential) when her child leaves home is to be an uninvolved parent in the first place, which makes no sense at all. The best you can do is to anticipate the situation and be prepared. As children need you less during the teen years, you can start to devote more time to your own interests. You can start to rebuild your life outside the home, both socially and vocationally. If you have fallen behind in job skills, you can get to work building them back up. And while we are on the topic, I would spend exactly zero time contemplating where you might be career-wise or income-wise if you hadn't taken the job of parenting so seriously. That decision reflected your values when you made it, and, at least from my perspective, it was the right one. Everyone is replaceable at a job. No one is replaceable as a parent.

Do not expect to get universal support as you recalibrate your life for this phase, by the way. Everyone is used to your being on call for whatever whenever. They will not be happy that you are less available. And you yourself may feel guilty. But this too is part of a process, and in the long run, it prepares everyone for their new roles. Teens can learn to do their own laundry, keep track of their own appointments, and clean up after themselves. (So can your spouse.) No matter what your child decides to do next, you do not want to be an enabler of childish behavior.

But don't take my word for it. Here are Sue's thoughts, a mom who is in the middle of the process:

Add "wings" to the list of things no one warns you about when you are planning to have children. My main purpose in life has been to nurture and protect these two human beings that I love more than anything on the planet. Now I have to release them into the world, kick them out of the nest, hoping they can fly on their own. I have to tell them with conviction and a brave face that it is time to go to college or work, be independent, and live on their own while my heart is breaking and all I really want to do is go back to the days of play dates and juice boxes. It is the loss of control and the uncertainty of knowing whether I have prepared my kids to tackle the rest of their journey that is so daunting. My logical mind knows letting them go is the end-game, the right thing to do, but my heart hurts.

Also, I feel the way we raise kids today has us attached from the hip at birth. We are always with them, taking them to play dates, supervising their outdoor play, attending their games, protecting them from the bad people in the world. Fear is a huge part of parenting now. I feel we were more independent as kids — more self-sufficient. There is an endless amount of risk out there, which may have existed when we were kids, but it's in your face from every form of media all the time. It almost feels like you are being neglectful letting your kid go out on their own in the world that the media portrays, and that adds to the anxiety of letting go.

Parenthetically, if you listen carefully to Sue, you can hear part of the impact of the internet on today's parents. Every fear is magnified. Every horrible story is posted and tweeted and retweeted. And, of course, everybody, after spreading the latest horrible story, posts a tissue of lies about the perfection of their own lives. Most of the parents I work with would be better off if they closed their Facebook accounts while they were actively parenting, and reopened them only to post pictures of sunsets after they retire. If at all. But I digress.

This "letting go" process is important both for teens who are on their way to college and for those who are headed into the workforce. In either case, no one keeps track of you. Let's start with kids going to college. When kids fail, it is often for the simplest of reasons: they don't turn off their electronics and go to bed. They don't get up in time for early classes. They don't eat regularly, and they don't plan their time effectively and get their homework done. I often watch parents micromanage the lives of their high school seniors and wonder what they expect to happen in September. Some kids acquire the necessary skills naturally. Some do not. By the senior year of high school, you certainly know which type you have. And if you have the "do not" type, it's an expensive gamble with a low frequency of success to simply send him off to college and hope somehow that things will be different.

On its face, the solution to this is simple: in the tenth through twelfth grade years, taper the amount of parental control and structure. Systematically cut back on checking with teachers, ensuring homework is passed in, and the many other interventions that may have been necessary through the years. This will have one of two results: 1) the child will take more responsibility for her own work, resulting in the development of skills that will transfer to college, or 2) grades will go down, as the child reveals that she is unwilling or unable (or some combination of the two) to achieve top results on her own.

It is the latter of these two possibilities, of course, that strikes fear into the hearts of a generation of parents who have come to believe that the college to which their child is admitted is the single most important outcome in their lives. (The question of how we arrived at this juncture is interesting — but not the business of our work here. However, were you to force me to give an opinion, I might say this: where your child goes to college is unlikely to be in the top ten important outcomes in his life, let alone at the top of the list.) These parents micro-manage their children's lives up until the minute they depart for college, often including the application process itself. This simply makes no sense. Let me, once again, point out the obvious: if your child is not ready to work independently by his senior year in high school, what do you suppose will be the result when no one is checking on him at college? If you are still having to force him to turn off his Xbox and go to bed, and still having to drag him out of that bed in time for school in the morning, how do you imagine that all this will hap-pen at college when you aren't there? The point is not to "get your child in" to the most competitive and prestigious college possible — although that seems to have become the ethos of today's America. The point is to help him find the appropriate next step after high school, and to go there armed with the requisite skills to succeed. If he needs a year between high school and college to grow up, so be it. That's a lot better than finding out in October of his freshman year that he wasn't ready to go — and having paid tuition to gain that knowledge. There's nothing like working a minimum wage job for a year to sharpen the senses about the need to acquire more than the minimum qualifications.

Let me give you an example. I'm currently working with the family of a tenth-grade boy, who has shown marginal motiva-tion to improve his grades, and whose family has provided both a peer tutor and a professional tutor, along with their own efforts to stay in touch with teachers about missing work, quiz and test grades, and so forth. The current plan is to start the junior year with the same interventions and then cut them back systematically during the year, so that he is essentially on his own by the start of senior year. The risk, of course, is that his grades — not particularly impressive in the first place — will go down. Our job, quietly and consistently, is to remind him that if this happens, he will have fewer options when high school ends. The harder he works, the more options he'll have. We do not, in the final analysis, want to save him from the consequences of his own action (or inaction). If he doesn't get into a demanding, competitive college, so what? He doesn't belong there. Better to go to a school well suited for who you are than to fail at one that sounds better to other parents.

Let's assume the best: your child slowly takes over the tasks of organization and planning, gets into college, and graduates from high school. The best preparation for college in the months before college actually starts is, of course, a summer job. It continues a level of structure, and a certain degree of systematic demands, that comprise a good preparation for the challenges to come. (I listen sometimes to eighteen-year-old young adults explain that they don't have a job, because their parents decided to "give them one last summer off." This is a horrible idea.) Also, in August, it's time to gradually move to a wake/sleep schedule that roughly resembles the plan for college. As noted elsewhere, it is frequently the simple things that spell the difference between success and failure on the first journey away from home. Getting enough sleep is one of them.

But what if the worst happens, and he doesn't get into college and leave home (or even worse than that, leaves home, fails, and has to come back)? Excellent question. And an excellent idea to have thought it out and talked about it long before it has a chance of happening. Here's the answer: high school graduates (or dropouts, for that matter) who are over the age of eighteen and live in your home are adult guests. Your provision of food and shelter for them is a gift — a product of your generosity. They do not have a right to it. This sounds simple, but it isn't. In fact, it's a radical change for everyone involved. Young adults who have returned home (or not left) frequently expect to have no rules at all. And access to a car. And money. Their parents, who may themselves feel a sense of guilt or shame that their child hasn't moved along or sympathy that college didn't work out, frequently provide all of this. I understand why people do it. But it's a bad idea.

Notice, by the way, that we are now also discussing the situation in which the child never left home in the first place. If your child never intended to go to college and got a job (or is intending to get a job) after high school, you still may be faced with a complex situation. And all of the questions in that last paragraph apply. What are the rules? What are the expectations? You do neither yourself nor your child any good by not discussing these issues. And you don't want to wake up in five years and wish you had.

The fact is, we *want* our young adults to move along to the next phase of their lives. We want home to be welcoming — but temporary. We want them to be comfortable — but not *too* comfortable. We want them to want to get up and out of there. How do we do this? In the broadest sense, we simply define what constitutes a healthy lifestyle: "You may stay here, but if you do so, you have to live a healthy lifestyle." Specifically, we might say the following: 1) get a job; 2) go to bed at a reasonable hour, and get up at a reasonable hour in the morning; 3) don't play video games for more than an hour or two a day; 4) don't smoke or drink (if he's under twenty-one); and 5) pay for your own gas and insurance, if you are using a family car. Maybe, in the longer run, 6) pay a nominal rent. As the parent, you are up to two things here. On the one hand, you are creating a system that incentivizes behavior that will support success. On the other, you are encouraging the notion that for your child to be truly free, he has to get out. And there is an element of self-interest for you as well. As the homeowner (not the proprietor of a cheap hotel), *you* can make rules that work for *you*. If you want to go to bed, but can't get to sleep until everyone is home, then make a curfew that meets that need.

Your child won't like this. He'll say that he's eighteen, a legal adult, and doesn't have to follow your rules. And he's right. But that works both ways. The way for him to "not have to follow your rules" is to move out. However, as an adult guest, the choice to stay is the choice to follow the rules. Establishing clarity on these issues in advance avoids the "I can't put my own son out on the streets" discussions that are torture for everyone involved. Words matter, and it's an entirely different thing to say, "If you don't follow the rules, I'll kick you out" than it is to say, "You absolutely have the right to not follow my rules, but if you choose to do that, you are choosing to move out." Don't wait until there's a rule infraction to have the discussion.

Returning to the college question, we should note that even if your child does successfully go off to school, the "letting go" question is still relevant. How often do you text or call? Do you access her grades in real time, the way you may have done in high school? I have known parents who, worried that their child won't get up for class, give wakeup calls. This won't work. If you have to do that, she's not ready to be there. There's a balance to be struck here, so let's take the questions one at a time. How often to text or call? About once a week. A little more for some kids, and a little less for others. You don't want to hover. (There's a reason for the term "helicopter parent." You don't want to be one.) You want to foster independence. As tempted as you might be to solve her problems, that's not the point of this phase. As we noted above, you want *her* to solve the problem, and then call to tell you how she did it. Talk less. Listen more.

The issue of grades is different. You are paying for this education, and you have a right to know if you are getting your money's worth. It may surprise you to know that you do not have an automatic right to see those grades, but that is the case. Your child is now eighteen and a legal adult. So as odd as it seems, even though you are paying the bill, your child has to give you "permission" to access the online grades, course information, etc. And you will insist that he does this. No compromises here. You no longer have daily contact and

141

access to teachers, and you are trying not to hover. So a dip in grades may be your first sign that something is up. Remember Taylor, from back in the Gaming section? You don't want to make the mistake his parents made. (As a side note, the same issue arises about medical treatment. When you drop your child off at college, take him by the Health Center, and get him to sign release forms that let the medical personnel talk to you.)

Here's something you don't want to hear: having a child come back home after a failed attempt at college is a lot more common than you think. After all that bragging about where their kid got in, it's not something parents like to talk about very much. And whatever the underlying reasons may be, the surface level reasons are usually straightforward: the kids don't eat properly, get enough sleep, go to class, work out, and do their homework. Sometimes they drink or smoke too much. Often, they don't control their use of electronics (whether it's gaming, social media, or whatever other distraction presents itself). Bottom line: they weren't ready to go in the first place.

If this happens to you, it's not the end of the world. A return home doesn't have to be ignominious. In fact, as we noted above, nothing does a better job at teaching a young adult about why she doesn't want to spend her life working at minimum wage than working for a year at minimum wage. As long as her parents don't make it too comfortable. Which you absolutely don't want to do. You can be kind. You can be empathic. But you do not want your young adult to settle into a life of no demands and no schedule. She gets a job, with

142

a regular schedule. She pays some bills. If she can handle it, she takes a class or two at a community college. She builds the work habits that will translate into success at whatever she does next. And most of all, she lives a healthy lifestyle as an adult guest in your home. A temporary adult guest, who wants to get out as soon as she is able.

And that's it.

Well, of course that's not really it. Even after they move out, we still care, and we still worry. But there's not much left we can control — and not much left we should control, even if we could. Somewhere down the road, they'll have enough perspective to make a judgment on the job we did. With any luck, they'll keep it to themselves. If they decide we did it wrong, that's ok. They can do it differently. We just want to be able to say that we thought it through, stuck with them through all the tears and all the laughter, and did the best job we could figure out to do. That's the contract. Good luck.

Appendix
How and When to Find Professional Help

Of course, sometimes even the best plans don't work. Maybe you have an extraordinarily difficult child. Maybe you're divorced, and a significant portion of your child's life is not in your control. Maybe you can't step back from your own life sufficiently: you know there's a problem, but you can't sort out how you're contributing. And maybe the problems are serious enough that you know for certain you need professional help (e.g., cutting, eating issues, and any sort of self-destructive behavior). Well, that's what mental health professionals are for.

The best way to find someone is a personal reference. If you have a friend who has used and liked someone, try that out. Pediatricians and their nurse practitioners are also excellent resources. Often, they've worked with a number of professionals and have good ideas. If you can't find a personal reference, go to the website of your health insurance, see who's covered in your area, and make some phone calls. The truth is, it's not always easy to find someone who sees children or adolescents. You have to be persistent, and you might have to go on some waiting lists.

This next part is my opinion, and some would disagree with me. What you're looking for usually isn't as much the specific credential or technique the professional uses, as that person's ability to form a relationship with your child. The relationship is the lever that the therapist uses to get change, and without it, all the technique in the world won't help. It just doesn't work to drag a kid to therapy week after week, just because someone told you that you should. What I say to parents who, for example, tell me that their teen needs help, but is reluctant to come, is this: tell him he only needs to come three times. If, at that point, he thinks it's stupid or a waste of time, then he doesn't need to come anymore. Truth is, if there isn't the start of a therapeutic alliance underway after three hours, it's probably not going to work anyway. Try someone else, or try again later. Unless, of course, there's suicidality involved. In which case, you're not waiting until later.

About the Author

Dr. James Mehegan is a Clinical Psychologist with a private practice located in Plymouth, MA. He graduated from Haverford College in 1974 with majors in German and Psychology. For the next three years, he was a full-time teacher, coach, and houseparent at Choate Rosemary Hall, a residential high school in Wallingford, Connecticut. In September of 1977, he enrolled in the Clinical Psychology program at Boston University, graduating with a Ph.D. in January of 1982. From 1982 to 1986, Dr. Mehegan lived in St. Croix in the U.S. Virgin Islands, where he taught windsurfing and tennis, but also opened a private practice, consulted to schools, taught at the College of the Virgin Islands, and was a Staff Psychologist at Charles Harwood Hospital in Christiansted.

In 1986, Dr. Mehegan was hired by the Department of Defense and moved to NATO Headquarters in Belgium to coordinate psychological services for the children of U.S. military and diplomatic personnel in Northern Europe. In 1989, he returned to the United States, where he opened a private practice. From 1991 to 2016, Dr. Mehegan was the Director of Counseling at Tabor Academy, a residential high school in Marion, MA.

Dr. Mehegan has also been a Scoutmaster, Girl Scout Leader, and coach of innumerable youth sports teams. He lives in Duxbury, MA, where he raised his three children with his wife of thirty-seven years, Diane.